Music Publishing

Music Publishing: The Roadmap to Royalties is an invaluable guide to generating and protecting royalties and geared toward emerging songwriters and artists. Music publishing—the business of acquiring copyrights and promoting, protecting, and collecting the royalties for music—generates the largest source of income for songwriters and composers. Taking a practical approach, the authors—one a successful music publisher and attorney, the other a songwriter and music business professor—explain in simple terms the basic concepts of the music publishing industry from a songwriter's point of view. They then break down the sources of income that can be exploited, examine the role of the music publisher, and then examine typical music publishing agreements, pointing out areas that writers need to review carefully. The book provides unique REALWORLD and MYTH-BUSTER sections, offering true, contemporary examples of successes and failures in the world of music publishing. The book reveals how millions of dollars have been earned—and lost—through the management of publishing rights.

Every serious emerging songwriter and artist will find *Music Publishing* invaluable in navigating the incredible opportunities and practical challenges that face music-makers in today's highly competitive and highly technological environment.

Ron Sobel is an entertainment attorney, with more than thirty years of experience representing songwriters, artists, and music companies. In 2001, Ron founded North Star Media (NSM), a music services and consulting company. Prior to NSM, Ron was V.P./Creative Affairs and head of the L.A. office at ASCAP. Ron was on the Board of Directors of the California Copyright Conference for eighteen years, and is a frequent speaker at colleges and universities.

Dick Weissman taught for twelve years in the Music & Entertainment Industry program at the University of Colorado at Denver, where he is Professor Emeritus, was V.P. for the Music & Entertainment Industry Educators Association, and has a long-term career as a studio musician, recording artist, songwriter, and record producer. He has written *Guitar Tunings and Blues: The Basics* for Routledge. He is also the coauthor of *The Global Music Industry*, *Promoting Your Music*, and *The Great Family Songbook*, also from Routledge.

Music Publishing
The Roadmap to Royalties

Ron Sobel and Dick Weissman

Routledge
Taylor & Francis Group

NEW YORK AND LONDON

First published 2008
by Routledge
270 Madison Ave, New York, NY 10016

Simultaneously published in the UK
by Routledge
2 Park Square, Milton Park, Abingdon, Oxon OX14 4RN

Routledge is an imprint of the Taylor & Francis Group, an informa business

Transferred to Digital Printing 2010

© 2008 Taylor & Francis

Typeset in Sabon by
Book Now Limited, London

Library of Congress Cataloging in Publication Data
Sobel, Ron.
Music publishing: the roadmap to royalties / Ron Sobel and Dick Weissman.
    p. cm.
1. Music publishing—United States. 2. Music—Economic aspects.
I. Weissman, Dick. II. Title.

ML112.S63 2008
070.5'794—dc22   2007050584

ISBN10: 0–415–97620–0 (hbk)
ISBN10: 0–415–97621–9 (pbk)
ISBN10: 0–203–89568–1 (ebk)

ISBN13: 978–0–415–97620–6 (hbk)
ISBN13: 978–0–415–97621–3 (pbk)
ISBN13: 978–0–203–89568–9 (ebk)

Contents

Figures

Foreword

There are dozens and dozens of books available for songwriters, and more than a half dozen books on music publishing. Some of them are quite useful, but generally speaking, you have to be a lawyer, have an unusual attention span, or have an MBA degree in order to understand them. When it's appropriate, we will recommend a few of these books. Our book, however, looks at the business of song-writing, royalties, and music publishing from a songwriter's point of view, and provides practical guidelines on the opportunities and challenges that every songwriter faces. But first, a little bit about us. Books about music publishing are usually written either by publishers or by songwriters. We are both of the above. Ron Sobel is a long-time Los Angeles resident and an entertainment industry attorney. Following years of private practice in entertainment law, Ron joined ASCAP (American Society of Composers, Authors, and Publishers) in 1986 as Director of Business Affairs, in the Los Angeles office. Ron worked at ASCAP for sixteen years, most recently as V.P./Creative Affairs, and head of the Los Angeles office, where he directed the twenty-one-member staff at ASCAP/L.A., and was a member of ASCAP's New Media Council. Ron signed Pearl Jam, Lenny Kravitz, Alice In Chains, Soundgarden, Dave Mason, and others to the company.

Today, Ron is President/Founder of North Star Media, a music publishing, administration, and consulting company based in Studio City, California. North Star Media (NSM) acquisitions include the prestigious Basically Gasp music catalogue (John/Bruce Hornsby), the Rhythm Fish/Jamm music catalogues (more than 350 titles, including Rod Stewart, Bonnie Raitt, Cher, Manhattan Transfer hits), and MusicBlitz Records (featuring recordings by Taj Mahal, Toots & The Maytals, Coolio, Pete Droge). NSM is actively engaged in representing writers and their catalogues in the film and television community, with recent music placements with The GAP, Kellogg's, Burger King, Verizon, Lexus, and at ABC, CBS, NBC, HBO, Fox Sports, Paramount Pictures, and Warner Brothers Pictures. Current consulting clients include American Honda Motors, American Idol/ Fremantle Entertainment, and the Alan Ett Creative Group. Ron was a fourteen-year member of the Board of Directors of the California Copyright Conference, and is a frequent lecturer at UCLA and USC.

Dick Weissman has, for a brief period, published his own music, but his expertise is as a songwriter and composer of instrumental music. Because he was involved in the folk-pop band, The Journeymen, during the 1960s, he is something of a scholar in regard to folk songs in the public domain. He is also a songwriter and composer of instrumental music, who has written many recorded songs, two feature film scores, and music for the theater and special events. He was a staff writer for two different publishers based in New York. He has also been active as the author of instructional materials for a number of music print publishers, including Alfred Music, Mel Bay Publications, and Cherry Lane Music.

In this book we will cover the history of music publishing and copyright, describe how the music publishing industry has evolved, and talk about what music publishers do in the modern world. Along the way we will discuss the lucrative income streams that filter to the songwriter and publisher from the virtually unlimited uses of music which fuel contemporary entertainment, art, and media.

Although we will focus on the American marketplace, we will also briefly discuss some of the key international markets, and some of the key differences between the royalty streams that writers enjoy in the United States and in other parts of the world.

Please note that throughout this book, it is our intention to equally include and refer to "he" writers and "she" writers, as well as "songwriters" and "composers." The words are to be considered interchangeable, as all music creators are equal opportunity royalty earners.

And finally, whenever possible, we strongly recommend that a qualified music lawyer should be consulted before any music agreement is signed. With the right counsel and bargaining power, you should be able to land smarter, better deals.

Ron Sobel and Dick Weissman

Introduction

Music Publishing—the business of acquiring copyrights and promoting, protecting, and collecting the royalties for millions of songs throughout the world—generates the largest source of income for songwriters and composers. With well over *nine billion dollars a year* (CISAC, 2005) flowing to songwriters and publishers throughout the world, the U.S. Copyright Act (Title 17, U.S. Code) establishes the foundation of laws and rights which serve as the roadmap for monetizing the ownership of creative works in the United States. And not unlike the U.S. tax code, copyright laws can be seen as a complex set of guidelines, fraught with arcane terminology and technical authorizations. This book provides practical explanations of the seemingly complicated world of music publishing, examines the relationship between a songwriter and publisher, and offers practical, easy-to-follow advice on taking songs to a lucrative global marketplace.

REALWORLD, MYTH-BUSTER, and !

Throughout the chapters in this book, we will highlight small passages about actual writers and their contracts, in order to clarify, amplify, and identify the pitfalls and opportunities inherent in various music publishing scenarios. Only the names have been changed. REALWORLD passages are exactly that—factual accounts of real writers and their deals. MYTH-BUSTER passages are exactly that—the de-bunking of rumors, myths, and music lore. And ! passages include those incontrovertible publishing axioms that should be fully understood before proceeding to the next chapter.

1 A brief history of music publishing and copyright law

In an historic U.S. Supreme Court decision, Justice Sandra Day O'Connor wrote that copyright protection—far from being inconsistent with the rights of free speech and freedom of information—is the very engine of free expression (Harper & Row, Publishers, Inc., et al. v. Nation Enterprises et al.; May 20, 1985). This principle is not new. Over 200 years ago, Benjamin Franklin, Thomas Jefferson, James Madison, and the other champions of American democracy, considered copyright protection and the ownership of intellectual property so essential and complementary to freedom of speech that they included a mandate for it in Article 1, Section 8 of the U.S. Constitution.

> Art. 1, Section 8. The Congress shall have power to . . . promote the progress of science and useful arts, by securing for limited times to authors and inventors the exclusive right to their respective writings and discoveries.

A brief history of copyright

Copyright was an inevitable extension of the creation of the printing press, and the use of moveable type. The invention of the press dates back to 1450, but the first printed music dates to 1495, and the world history book revised by Wynkyn de Worde in London. Details of the evolution of music copyright and the process of printing music are available in Russell Sanjek's groundbreaking book, *American Popular Music and its Business: The First Four Hundred Years, Volume 1, The Beginning to 1790*. Among the many stones along the path, Sanjek dates the use of lute tablature to 1508. Lute tablature, the ancestor of guitar tablature, is a system of indicating notes through the use of numbers or diagrams.

In 1790 the United States Congress passed a federal copyright act, but it did not protect music. Publishers got around this omission by publishing music books, and protecting them as books, rather than as original musical compositions. The initial term of protection was fourteen years. A copyright could be renewed, but only one renewal was permitted. If a copyright was not renewed, it would fall into the *public domain*. Works in the public domain do not belong to a composer or publisher, but are freely available for use by anyone. Many folksongs, for example, are in the public domain, because we do not know who the original author was, and often these works had never been formally published or copyrighted.

It is important to note that at this point in time, authors or songwriters received a single payment for their work, and royalties were unknown. The only recourse that a songwriter had was to take on the additional task of publication, as well as authorship. Copyright has grown from a legal concept regulating copying rights in the publishing of books and maps to one with a significant effect on nearly every modern industry, covering such items as sound recordings, films, photographs, software, and architectural works. We will return to this thread of thought when we undertake a discussion of songwriters or composers who own their own publishing companies.

The Berne Convention

The 1866 Berne Convention first established recognition of copyrights among sovereign nations. Under the Berne Convention, copyrights for creative works do not have to be asserted or declared, as they are automatically in force at creation: an author need not "register" or "apply for" a copyright in countries adhering to the Berne Convention. As soon as a work is "fixed," that is, written or recorded on some physical medium, its author is automatically entitled to all copyrights in the work, and to any derivative works unless and until the author explicitly disclaims them, or until the copyright expires. The United States did not sign the Berne Convention until 1989. Currently 160 nations have signed on to the Berne Convention.

Music publishers and sheet music

Up until the early part of the twentieth century, the music publishing business was primarily involved in publishing printed sheet music. The bulk of its income came from the sales of printed sheet music, and the sheet music was promoted by convincing popular performers to sing a new song. In return, the artist, as we will see later, was compensated in various ways. All sorts of inventive ploys were used to help promote songs. Publishers hired people to get up and yell out requests for new songs, and sometimes claques of people were paid small amounts of money to loudly applaud performances of a publisher's music. And payola did not begin with the rock and roll business of the 1950s, but was practiced in nineteenth-century England, when publishers sometimes paid performers to perform songs. Songwriters received royalties primarily from the sales of sheet music. No income was generated from musical performances, early recordings did not mandate any licensing fees for the use of songs on records, and radio did not exist until the 1920s. Prior to the advent of radio, published songs were promoted through performances and endorsements by the popular performers of the day. Often the performer's name and picture would appear on the cover of the sheet music, for which the performer was paid a fee or even given a composer credit. If the song became popular, the performer would, in essence, share in the royalties with the songwriter or songwriters.

The nature of copyright

By ensuring that creators are fairly compensated for the use of their works, strong copyright laws encourage the broadest possible participation of citizens in the creative process. Compensation for the use of copyrighted works enables those whose works the public deems of value to continue creating, while encouraging newcomers with something to say to join in. The national and global culture is enormously enriched by such a system, which rewards the most popular and talented creators and allows them to devote themselves full time to their art. Great works engender increased public discussion, and the creation of new art, to the betterment of all. By the same token, without adequate copyright protections and enforcement, the fruits of human creativity are severely diminished. Uncompensated creators are not afforded the time, the resources, or other incentives to create. After a while, the well of great new works runs dry. The notion is the same as that underlying all property rights: with ownership comes the right to control use.

Copyright law

The grants established by the Copyright Act serve to create ownership rights—*intellectual property rights*—in the creative works of authors, lyricists, songwriters, and composers. Much like ownership rights in real estate and other personal property, songs created from the "factory of the mind" are valuable property assets that can generate substantial wealth, and can lead to long-lasting careers. And like other more traditional property rights, interests in copyrights can be sold, licensed, assigned, and passed on to the owners' heirs. Legally, a copyright means that a musician, author, or artist has a "limited duration monopoly" on anything she creates. The U.S. Constitution grants the government power "to promote the progress of science and useful arts, by securing for limited times to authors and inventors the exclusive right to their respective writings and discoveries" (Article 1 Section 8, U.S. Constitution).

Copyright law covers only the form or manner in which ideas or information have been manifested, the "form of material expression." It is not designed or intended to cover the actual ideas, concepts, facts, styles, or techniques which may be embodied in or represented by the copyright work—this is called the idea/expression or fact/expression dichotomy. Copyright is a set of exclusive rights regulating the use of a particular expression of an idea or information. At its most general, it is literally "the right to copy" an original creation. For example, if a writer has a general concept or idea for a song, a copyright of that "idea" does not prohibit other writers from creating the same general idea for a project. However, if the writer develops the idea to a point of detailed and specific lyric and melody, then that specific expression of the idea is copyrighted. Copyright may subsist in a wide range of creative, intellectual, or artistic forms or "works." These include musical compositions, audio recordings, and radio and television broadcasts of live and other performances. Copyright is one of the laws covered by the umbrella term "intellectual property." In most cases, these rights are of limited duration. The symbol for copyright is ©, and in some jurisdictions may alternatively be written as (c).

Writer share and publisher share

> ❗ It is fundamental to understand that when a writer or composer creates a work, whether alone or with others, the writer(s) owns that entire song and all of the rights—both the so-called "writer's half" and the so-called "publisher's half" of the work—for the full term afforded by copyright protection. One hundred percent of the rights in a song, and 100 percent of the royalties, are owned by the writer . . . until such time as the writer voluntarily agrees to sell or assign a "publisher's" interest in the work to a publisher. It is this basic principle of 100 percent writer ownership that underlies all copyright ownership rights, transactions, and royalties.

This principle cannot be overstated. A song, when first written, is owned entirely by its writer(s). A music publisher obtains its interest and rights in a song only when the writer chooses to enter into a written contract granting an assignment of a portion of the song, up to 50 percent of the entire song (the "publisher's half"), in exchange for providing either money or services (Chapter 5). Other than the unique situation wherein a writer is engaged to create a "work-for-hire" (Chapter 7), a songwriter generally retains ownership of at least 50 percent of the song (the "writer's half"), and can choose to sell or barter up to 50 percent of the remainder of the song (the "publisher's half") in order to engage the services of a publisher (see Figure 1.1). A writer, of course, always has the option of retaining all of the song rights, without ever engaging an outside publisher. Equally important, however, is the clear fact that some songwriters may not have the skills, knowledge, or desire to adequately serve as their own music publisher (Chapter 4).

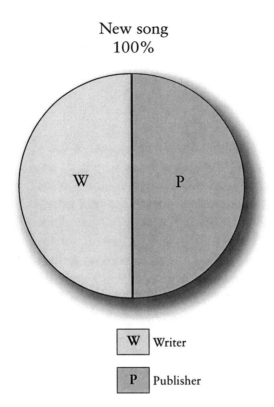

New song
100%

W

P

W | Writer

P | Publisher

Figure 1.1 Writer share and publisher share.

Inherent rights of "copyright"

Under section 106 of the Copyright Act, and subject to some limitations (Chapter 12), the copyright owner is granted the exclusive right to do five specific activities, and is, therefore, authorized to collect five sources of royalty income generated through sales and licensing of the song, including:

1. the right to reproduce the copyrighted work in copies or phonorecords; to produce copies or reproductions of the work and to sell those copies (including, typically, electronic copies);
2. the right to prepare derivative works based upon the copyrighted work; to create derivative works (works that adapt the original work);
3. the right to distribute copies or phonorecords of the copy-

righted work to the public by sale or other transfer of ownership;
4. the right to perform the copyrighted work publicly;
5. the right to exhibit the copyrighted work publicly.

These provisions of the Copyright Act apply to songwriters, composers, and publishers. Although recording artists have several
other lucrative means of generating royalties and income, the
focus of this book is primarily on the rights and income opportunities for songwriters, composers, and music publishers. Each of
the five provisions in the Act grants exclusive ownership rights,
and authorizes specific activities for the songwriter. The phrase
"exclusive right" means that only the copyright holder is free to
exercise these rights, and others are prohibited from using the
work without the consent of the copyright holder. In practical
terms, each of these activities can generate tens, if not hundreds
of thousands, of dollars to the owner(s) of the copyright. And
with one exception—statutory mechanical rates—all of the rights
allowing use of a work, together with the fees that can be
charged, are negotiable and totally within the control of the copyright owner. All of the legal rights, and therefore, income, that
flow from a song to its songwriters and publishers originate with
the rights established in the U.S. Copyright Act. One of the most
unique aspects of copyright ownership is the fact that a successful
song can often generate more than thirty different royalty streams,
including income from television and radio airplay ("performance income"), sales of records and CDs ("mechanical income"),
and uses in a film or commercial ("synchronization income").
Each of these revenue streams will be examined in later chapters.
    The five provisions of the Copyright Act are:

1. *The owner of a copyright in a song has the exclusive right
   to reproduce or authorize the reproduction of the song in
   phonorecords, CDs, digital formats ("mechanical royalties")
   or in copies, which include motion picture, television production, and commercials ("synchronization royalties"):*

   A. Mechanical royalties are those monies paid by a record
   company to a writer and publisher for the right ("mechanical
   license") to manufacture and *reproduce* "mechanical" versions (albums and CDs) of a song. This statutory mechanical

royalty rate (9.1 cents/song, in 2007) is the only non-nego-
tiable (compulsory) license fee established by the Copyright
Act. All of the other rights and fees are completely negotiable.
Following the initial authorized publication, all others can
record and distribute a version of the work by complying
with the statutory procedures of the "compulsory license"
provisions of the copyright act, which require payment of the
statutory royalty rate to the publisher.

> ❗ The mechanical royalty income is split among the "writer's
> half" and the "publisher's half". A million-selling single, at 9.1
> cents/song × 1,000,000 units, generates $91,000.00 for the 100
> percent mechanical royalty payment. With $45,500.00 going to
> the writer, and $45,500.00 going to the publisher, the writer's
> decision to enter into a publishing contract has very substantial
> financial impacts.

B. Synchronization royalties are those monies paid to the
owner of a copyright for the right to use a song when reproduced and synchronized in an audio-visual presentation.
Unlike the statutory mechanical rate, the synchronization
license and fee is entirely negotiable, and can be restricted or
denied entirely by the copyright owner. The use of music in
film and television has become increasingly more important
to the success of a production, and therefore, more lucrative
to the copyright owners. As CD and record sales have
decreased, the number of productions, independent producers, and cable and satellite outlets has dramatically
increased. The growing opportunity to place music in these
productions provides writers and publishers with an ever-
expanding market to license their works.

2. *The copyright owner has the exclusive right to prepare, or
   authorize others to prepare a Derivative Work based upon
   the copyrighted work*:

A Derivative Work is a subsequent work, such as a translation, music arrangement, or motion picture version, which is

based upon a pre-existing work. This right allows the original copyright owner to maintain an on-going ownership interest in any subsequent revision, adaptation, or production which incorporates a portion of the original work. Depending on the nature and use of the original work, ownership interests in the derivative work can generate substantial licensing and on-going royalty income for the original copyright owner.

3. *The copyright owner has the exclusive right to distribute copies or phonorecords of the copyrighted work to the public by sale or other transfer of ownership*:

The owner of a copyright in a song has the exclusive right to make and *distribute* the initial release of the song to the public. Prior to the initial public distribution, the copyright owner can request any fee for a mechanical license, or can refuse outright to grant a mechanical license. The value of this distribution right is in the ability of the copyright owner to withhold the initial publication until the right project—and the right price—is offered. In practice, however, writers and publishers are generally happy to authorize use of their works to most of the recordings, licenses, and synchronizations that show interest in using the song.

4. *The owner of a copyright in a song has the exclusive right to perform the song publicly ("public performance royalties")*:

Performance royalties are those monies paid by parties who choose to use ("publicly perform") copyrighted songs in their establishments or properties. Copyright owners have the exclusive right to perform their own musical works in public. All others must enter into a licensing agreement to perform the music. Radio and television broadcasters, for example, are required to obtain the permission—and pay a fee—to songwriters and publishers for the right to use the works on their stations. More on performance rights in Chapter 3.

5. *The owner of a copyright in a song has the exclusive right to exhibit the copyrighted work publicly*:

This is the right to authorize others to display (project) copy-righted sheet music, or lyric reprints of a song.

In addition to these five specific statutory provisions, there is a broad and ever-evolving range of *ancillary royalties* which are derived from the exploitation of the copyrighted work in various other new and evolving markets, including digital downloads, and licensing for the new media markets of ringtones, callbacks, videogames, greeting cards, and karaoke performances.

Obtaining and enforcing copyright

Typically, a work must meet minimal standards of originality in order to qualify for copyright, and the copyright expires after a set period of time. In the United States, copyright has been made automatic (in the style of the Berne Convention) since March 1, 1989, which has had the effect of making it appear to be more like a property right. Thus, as with property, a copyright need not be granted or obtained through official registration with any government office. Once an idea has been reduced to tangible form, for example, by securing it in a fixed medium (such as a drawing, sheet music, photograph, a videotape, or a letter), the copyright holder is entitled to enforce his exclusive rights.

Copyright registration

The purpose of copyright registration is to place on record a verifiable account of the date and content of the work in question, so that in the event of a legal claim, or case of infringement or plagiarism, the copyright owner can produce a copy of the work from an independently verifiable source. While a copyright need not be officially registered for the copyright owner to begin exercising her exclusive rights, *registration of works* does have benefits; it serves as prima facie evidence of a valid copyright and enables the copyright holder to seek statutory damages and attorney's fees (whereas in the United States, for instance, registering after an infringement only enables one to receive actual damages and lost profits). It is a common misconception, therefore, to confuse copyright registration with the granting of copyright. To legally enforce an author's claim to his copyright, his work must be registered with the copyright office. Registering a composition provides public notification of copyright, prohibiting most public uses of the composition unless a license, permission, or payment of fees (royalties) has been arranged. If a song is used while under copyright without the owner's permission, the user is subject to legal repercussions.

The cost to register musical works in 2007 is $45.00, per song. According to the U.S. Copyright Office, U.S. Copyright Form PA (Performing Arts) is used to register the underlying musical composition or dramatic work, or for registration of published or unpublished works of the performing arts (see Figure 1.2). Works of the performing arts include: (1) musical works, including any accompanying words; (2) dramatic works, including any accompanying music.

U.S. Copyright Form SR (Sound Recording) is used to register the "sound recording" itself, but not the underlying musical or dramatic work (see Figure 1.3). Form SR has been developed specifically to register a "sound recording," separate and distinct from the underlying musical or dramatic work. File Form SR if you are the copyright claimant for both the underlying musical work and the sound recording, and you prefer to register both on the same form.

If the musical work to be registered has been recorded (as a tape or CD), either Form PA (Performing Arts) or Form SR (Sound Recording) may be used, depending on the purpose of the registration.

File both forms PA and SR if the copyright claimant for the underlying work and sound recording differ, or you prefer to have separate registrations for them.

It is not unusual for a songwriter to write and register several songs within a short period. At $45.00 per song, the costs of registering many songs can be expensive. The Copyright Office allows for the registration of a "collection" of songs, for a single $45.00 fee. It is suggested to write the name of each song on the collection CD prior to submission, in order to identify individual song titles at a later date. If one of the songs in the collection gets recorded, it is wise to copyright that song individually, under its own title, by completing Form CA: Correction and Amplification. The reason is that that particular song has some commercial value, and should anyone infringe it, you can easily prove that the song is registered in your name at the Library of Congress. You cannot register a collection of songs by a variety of authors. The applicant must have a credit as writer or co-writer on all the songs in the collection. The copyright office also offers a number of useful forms and pamphlets which are available at www.copyright.gov.

Form PA

Detach and read these instructions before completing this form.
Make sure all applicable spaces have been filled in before you return this form.

When to Use This Form: Use Form PA for registration of published or unpublished works of the performing arts. This class includes works prepared for the purpose of being "performed" directly before an audience or indirectly "by means of any device or process." Works of the performing arts include: (1) musical works, including any accompanying words; (2) dramatic works, including any accompanying music; (3) pantomimes and choreographic works; and (4) motion pictures and other audiovisual works.

Deposit to Accompany Application: An application for copyright registration must be accompanied by a deposit consisting of copies or phonorecords representing the entire work for which registration is made. The following are the general deposit requirements as set forth in the statute:

Unpublished Work: Deposit one complete copy (or phonorecord).

Published Work: Deposit two complete copies (or one phonorecord) of the best edition.

Work First Published Outside the United States: Deposit one complete copy (or phonorecord) of the first foreign edition.

Contribution to a Collective Work: Deposit one complete copy (or phonorecord) of the best edition of the collective work.

Motion Pictures: Deposit *both* of the following: (1) a separate written description of the contents of the motion picture; and (2) for a published work, one complete copy of the best edition of the motion picture; or, for an unpublished work, one complete copy of the motion picture or identifying material. Identifying material may be either an audiorecording of

the entire soundtrack or one frame enlargement or similar visual print from each 10-minute segment.

The Copyright Notice: Before March 1, 1989, the use of copyright notice was mandatory on all published works, and any work first published before that date should have carried a notice. For works first published on and after March 1, 1989, use of the copyright notice is optional. For more information about copyright notice, see Circular 3, *Copyright Notice.*

For Further Information: To speak to a Copyright Office staff member, call (202) 707-3000 (TTY: (202) 707-6737). Recorded information is available 24 hours a day. Order forms and other publications from the address in space 9 or call the Forms and Publications Hotline at (202) 707-9100. Access and download circulars, forms, and other information from the Copyright Office website at *www.copyright.gov.*

Please type or print using black ink. The form is used to produce the certificate.

1 SPACE 1: Title

Title of This Work: Every work submitted for copyright registration must be given a title to identify that particular work. If the copies or phonorecords of the work bear a title (or an identifying phrase that could serve as a title), transcribe that wording *completely* and *exactly* on the application. Indexing of the registration and future identification of the work will depend on the information you give here. If the work you are registering is an entire "collective work" (such as a collection of plays or songs), give the overall title of the collection. If you are registering one or more individual contributions to a collective work, give the title of each contribution, followed by the title of the collection. For an unpublished collection, you may give the titles of the individual works after the collection title.

Previous or Alternative Titles: Complete this space if there are any additional titles for the work under which someone searching for the registration might be likely to look, or under which a document pertaining to the work might be recorded.

Nature of This Work: Briefly describe the general nature or character of the work being registered for copyright. Examples: "Music"; "Song Lyrics"; "Words and Music"; "Drama"; "Musical Play"; "Choreography"; "Pantomime"; "Motion Picture"; "Audiovisual Work."

2 SPACE 2: Author(s)

General Instructions: After reading these instructions, decide who are the "authors" of this work for copyright purposes. Then, unless the work is a "collective work," give the requested information about every "author" who contributed any appreciable amount of copyrightable matter to this version of the work. If you need further space, request additional Continuation Sheets. In the case of a collective work such as a songbook or a collection of plays, give information about the author of the collective work as a whole.

Name of Author: The fullest form of the author's name should be given. Unless the work was "made for hire," the individual who actually created the work is its "author." In the case of a work made for hire, the statute provides that "the employer or other person for whom the work was prepared is considered the author."

What Is a "Work Made for Hire"? A "work made for hire" is defined as: (1) "a work prepared by an employee within the scope of his or her employment"; or (2) "a work specially ordered or commissioned for use as a contribution to a collective work, as a part of a motion picture or other audiovisual work, as a translation, as a supplementary work, as a compilation, as an instructional text, as a test, as answer material for a test, or as an atlas, if the parties expressly agree in a written instrument signed by them that the work shall be considered a work made for hire." If you have checked "Yes" to indicate that the work was "made for hire," you must give the full legal name of the employer (or other person for whom the work was prepared). You may also include the name of the employee along with the name of the employer (for example: "Elster Music Co., employer for hire of John Ferguson").

"Anonymous" or "Pseudonymous" Work: An author's contribution to a work is "anonymous" if that author is not identified on the copies or phonorecords of the work. An author's contribution to a work is "pseudonymous" if that author is identified on the copies or phonorecords under a fictitious name. If the work is "anonymous" you may: (1) leave the line blank; or (2) state "anonymous" on the line; or (3) reveal the author's identity. If the work is "pseudonymous" you may: (1) leave the line blank; or (2) give the pseudonym and identify it as such (example: "Huntley Haverstock, pseudonym"); or (3) reveal the author's name, making clear which is the real name and which is the pseudonym (for example: "Judith Barton, whose pseudonym is Madeline Elster"). However, the citizenship or domicile of the author *must* be given in all cases.

Dates of Birth and Death: If the author is dead, the statute requires that the year of death be included in the application unless the work is anonymous or pseudonymous. The author's birth date is optional, but is useful as a form of identification. Leave this space blank if the author's contribution was a "work made for hire."

Author's Nationality or Domicile: Give the country of which the author is a citizen, or the country in which the author is domiciled. Nationality or domicile *must* be given in all cases.

Nature of Authorship: Give a brief general statement of the nature of this particular author's contribution to the work. Examples: "Words", "Coauthor of Music"; "Words and Music"; "Arrangement"; "Coauthor of Book and Lyrics"; "Dramatization"; "Screen Play"; "Compilation and English Translation"; "Editorial Revisions."

Figure 1.2 Form PA (Performing Arts) page 1.

SPACE 3: Creation and Publication

General Instructions: Do not confuse "creation" with "publication." Every application for copyright registration must state "the year in which creation of the work was completed." Give the date and nation of first publication only if the work has been published.

Creation: Under the statute, a work is "created" when it is fixed in a copy or phonorecord for the first time. Where a work has been prepared over a period of time, the part of the work existing in fixed form on a particular date constitutes the created work on that date. The date you give here should be the year in which the author completed the particular version for which registration is now being sought, even if other versions exist or if further changes or additions are planned.

Publication: The statute defines "publication" as "the distribution of copies or phonorecords of a work to the public by sale or other transfer of ownership, or by rental, lease, or lending"; a work is also "published" if there has been an "offering to distribute copies or phonorecords to a group of persons for purposes of further distribution, public performance, or public display." Give the full date (month, day, year) when, and the country where, publication first occurred. If first publication took place simultaneously in the United States and other countries, it is sufficient to state "U.S.A."

SPACE 4: Claimant(s)

Name(s) and Address(es) of Copyright Claimant(s): Give the name(s) and address(es) of the copyright claimant(s) in this work even if the claimant is the same as the author. Copyright in a work belongs initially to the author of the work (including, in the case of a work made for hire, the employer or other person for whom the work was prepared). The copyright claimant is either the author of the work or a person or organization to whom the copyright initially belonging to the author has been transferred.

Transfer: The statute provides that, if the copyright claimant is not the author, the application for registration must contain "a brief statement of how the claimant obtained ownership of the copyright." If any copyright claimant named in space 4 is not an author named in space 2, give a brief statement explaining how the claimant(s) obtained ownership of the copyright. Examples: "By written contract"; "Transfer of all rights by author"; "Assignment"; "By will." Do not attach transfer documents or other attachments or riders.

SPACE 5: Previous Registration

General Instructions: The questions in space 5 are intended to show whether an earlier registration has been made for this work and, if so, whether there is any basis for a new registration. As a general rule, only one basic copyright registration can be made for the same version of a particular work.

Same Version: If this version is substantially the same as the work covered by a previous registration, a second registration is not generally possible unless: (1) the work has been registered in unpublished form and a second registration is now being sought to cover this first published edition; or (2) someone other than the author is identified as copyright claimant in the earlier registration, and the author is now seeking registration in his or her own name. If either of these two exceptions applies, check the appropriate box and give the earlier registration number and date. Otherwise, do not submit Form PA; instead, write the Copyright Office

for information about supplementary registration or recordation of transfers of copyright ownership.

Changed Version: If the work has been changed and you are now seeking registration to cover the additions or revisions, check the last box in space 5, give the earlier registration number and date, and complete both parts of space 6 in accordance with the instructions below.

Previous Registration Number and Date: If more than one previous registration has been made for the work, give the number and date of the latest registration.

SPACE 6: Derivative Work or Compilation

General Instructions: Complete space 6 if this work is a "changed version," "compilation," or "derivative work," and if it incorporates one or more earlier works that have already been published or registered for copyright or that have fallen into the public domain. A "compilation" is defined as "a work formed by the collection and assembling of preexisting materials or of data that are selected, coordinated, or arranged in such a way that the resulting work as a whole constitutes an original work of authorship." A "derivative work" is "a work based on one or more preexisting works." Examples of derivative works include musical arrangements, dramatizations, translations, abridgments, condensations, motion picture versions, or "any other form in which a work may be recast, transformed, or adapted." Derivative works also include works "consisting of editorial revisions, annotations, or other modifications" if these changes, as a whole, represent an original work of authorship.

Preexisting Material (space 6a): Complete this space *and* space 6b for derivative works. In this space identify the preexisting work that has been recast, transformed, or adapted. For example, the preexisting material might be: "French version of Hugo's 'Le Roi s'anuse'." Do not complete this space for compilations.

Material Added to This Work (space 6b): Give a brief, general statement of the *additional* new material covered by the copyright claim for which registration is sought. In the case of a derivative work, identify this new material. Examples: "Arrangement for piano and orchestra"; "Dramatization for television"; "New film version"; "Revisions throughout; Act III completely new." If the work is a compilation, give a brief, general statement describing both the material that has been compiled *and* the compilation itself. Example: "Compilation of 19th Century Military Songs."

 SPACE 7, 8, 9: Fee, Correspondence, Certification, Return Address

Deposit Account: If you maintain a Deposit Account in the Copyright Office, identify it in space 7a. Otherwise, leave the space blank and send the fee with your application and deposit.

Correspondence (space 7b): Give the name, address, area code, telephone number, fax number, and email address (if available) of the person to be consulted if correspondence about this application becomes necessary.

Certification (space 8): The application cannot be accepted unless it bears the date and the **handwritten signature** of the author or other copyright claimant, or of the owner of exclusive right(s), or of the duly authorized agent of the author, claimant, or owner of exclusive right(s).

Address for Return of Certificate (space 9): The address box must be completed legibly since the certificate will be returned in a window envelope.

 ▬▬▬ MORE INFORMATION ▬▬▬

How to Register a Recorded Work: If the musical or dramatic work that you are registering has been recorded (as a tape, disk, or cassette), you may choose either copyright application Form PA (Performing Arts) or Form SR (Sound Recordings), depending on the purpose of the registration.

Use Form PA to register the underlying musical composition or dramatic work. Form SR has been developed specifically to register a "sound recording" as defined by the Copyright Act—a work resulting from the "fixation of a series of sounds," separate and distinct from the underlying musical or dramatic work. Form SR should be used when the copyright claim is limited to the sound recording itself. (In one instance, Form SR may also be used to file for a copyright registration for both kinds of works—see (4) below.) Therefore:

(1) File Form PA if you are seeking to register the musical or dramatic work, not the "sound recording," even though what you deposit for copyright purposes may be in the form of a phonorecord.

(2) File Form PA if you are seeking to register the audio portion of an audiovisual work, such as a motion picture soundtrack; these are considered integral parts of the audiovisual work.

(3) File Form SR if you are seeking to register the "sound recording" itself, that is, the work that results from the fixation of a series of musical, spoken, or other sounds, but not the underlying musical or dramatic work.

(4) File Form SR if you are the copyright claimant for both the underlying musical or dramatic work and the sound recording, *and* you prefer to register both on the same form.

(5) File both forms PA and SR if the copyright claimant for the underlying work and sound recording differ, or you prefer to have separate registration for them.

"Copies" and "Phonorecords": To register for copyright, you are required to deposit "copies" or "phonorecords." These are defined as follows:

Musical compositions may be embodied (fixed) in "copies," objects from which a work can be read or visually perceived, directly or with the aid of a machine or device, such as manuscripts, books, sheet music, film, and videotape. They may also be fixed in "phonorecords," objects embodying fixations of sounds, such as tapes and phonograph disks, commonly known as phonograph records. For example, a song (the work to be registered) can be reproduced in sheet music ("copies") or phonograph records ("phonorecords"), or both.

Figure 1.2 Form PA (Performing Arts) page 2.

For best results, fill in the form on-screen and then print it.

Form PA
For a Work of Performing Arts
UNITED STATES COPYRIGHT OFFICE

REGISTRATION NUMBER

PA   PAU

EFFECTIVE DATE OF REGISTRATION

Month   Day   Year

DO NOT WRITE ABOVE THIS LINE. IF YOU NEED MORE SPACE, USE A SEPARATE CONTINUATION SHEET.

1

TITLE OF THIS WORK ▼

PREVIOUS OR ALTERNATIVE TITLES ▼

NATURE OF THIS WORK ▼ See instructions

2

a

NAME OF AUTHOR ▼

DATES OF BIRTH AND DEATH
Year Born ▼   Year Died ▼

Was this contribution to the work a "work made for hire"?
☐ Yes
☐ No

AUTHOR'S NATIONALITY OR DOMICILE
Name of Country
OR { Citizen of _____
{ Domiciled in _____

WAS THIS AUTHOR'S CONTRIBUTION TO THE WORK
Anonymous? ☐ Yes ☐ No
Pseudonymous? ☐ Yes ☐ No

If the answer to either of these questions is "Yes," see detailed instructions.

NATURE OF AUTHORSHIP Briefly describe nature of material created by this author in which copyright is claimed. ▼

NOTE

Under the law, the "author" of a "work made for hire" is generally the employer, not the employee (see instructions). For any part of this work that was "made for hire" check "Yes" in the space provided, give the employer (or other person for whom the work was prepared) as "Author" of that part, and leave the space for dates of birth and death blank.

b

NAME OF AUTHOR ▼

DATES OF BIRTH AND DEATH
Year Born ▼   Year Died ▼

Was this contribution to the work a "work made for hire"?
☐ Yes
☐ No

AUTHOR'S NATIONALITY OR DOMICILE
Name of Country
OR { Citizen of _____
{ Domiciled in _____

WAS THIS AUTHOR'S CONTRIBUTION TO THE WORK
Anonymous? ☐ Yes ☐ No
Pseudonymous? ☐ Yes ☐ No

If the answer to either of these questions is "Yes," see detailed instructions.

NATURE OF AUTHORSHIP Briefly describe nature of material created by this author in which copyright is claimed. ▼

c

NAME OF AUTHOR ▼

DATES OF BIRTH AND DEATH
Year Born ▼   Year Died ▼

Was this contribution to the work a "work made for hire"?
☐ Yes
☐ No

AUTHOR'S NATIONALITY OR DOMICILE
Name of Country
OR { Citizen of _____
{ Domiciled in _____

WAS THIS AUTHOR'S CONTRIBUTION TO THE WORK
Anonymous? ☐ Yes ☐ No
Pseudonymous? ☐ Yes ☐ No

If the answer to either of these questions is "Yes," see detailed instructions.

NATURE OF AUTHORSHIP Briefly describe nature of material created by this author in which copyright is claimed. ▼

3

a YEAR IN WHICH CREATION OF THIS WORK WAS COMPLETED
This information must be given in all cases.
Year

b DATE AND NATION OF FIRST PUBLICATION OF THIS PARTICULAR WORK
Complete this information ONLY if this work has been published.
Month _____ Day _____ Year _____
Nation

4

See instructions before completing this space.

COPYRIGHT CLAIMANT(S) Name and address must be given even if the claimant is the same as the author given in space 2. ▼

TRANSFER If the claimant(s) named here in space 4 is (are) different from the author(s) named in space 2, give a brief statement of how the claimant(s) obtained ownership of the copyright. ▼

APPLICATION RECEIVED

ONE DEPOSIT RECEIVED

TWO DEPOSITS RECEIVED

FUNDS RECEIVED

DO NOT WRITE HERE
OFFICE USE ONLY

MORE ON BACK ▶ • Complete all applicable spaces (numbers 5-9) on the reverse side of this page
• See detailed instructions. • Sign the form at line 8.

DO NOT WRITE HERE

Page 1 of _____ pages

Figure 1.2 Form PA (Performing Arts) page 3.

DO NOT WRITE ABOVE THIS LINE. IF YOU NEED MORE SPACE, USE A SEPARATE CONTINUATION SHEET.

PREVIOUS REGISTRATION Has registration for this work, or for an earlier version of this work, already been made in the Copyright Office?

☐ Yes ☐ No If your answer is "Yes," why is another registration being sought? (Check appropriate box.) ▼ If your answer is No, do not check box A, B, or C.

a. ☐ This is the first published edition of a work previously registered in unpublished form.

b. ☐ This is the first application submitted by this author as copyright claimant.

c. ☐ This is a changed version of the work, as shown by space 6 on this application.

If your answer is "Yes," give: **Previous Registration Number** ▼   **Year of Registration** ▼

5

DERIVATIVE WORK OR COMPILATION Complete both space 6a and 6b for a derivative work; complete only 6b for a compilation.

Preexisting Material Identify any preexisting work or works that this work is based on or incorporates. ▼

Material Added to This Work Give a brief, general statement of the material that has been added to this work and in which copyright is claimed. ▼

6 a b

See instructions before completing this space.

DEPOSIT ACCOUNT If the registration fee is to be charged to a Deposit Account established in the Copyright Office, give name and number of Account.

Name ▼   **Account Number** ▼

CORRESPONDENCE Give name and address to which correspondence about this application should be sent. Name/Address/Apt/City/State/Zip ▼

Area code and daytime telephone number   (   )   Fax number   (   )

Email

7 a b

CERTIFICATION* I, the undersigned, hereby certify that I am the

Check only one {
☐ author
☐ other copyright claimant
☐ owner of exclusive right(s)
☐ authorized agent of
}

Name of author or other copyright claimant, or owner of exclusive right(s) ▲

of the work identified in this application and that the statements made by me in this application are correct to the best of my knowledge.

Typed or printed name and date ▼ If this application gives a date of publication in space 3, do not sign and submit it before that date.

Date

Handwritten signature (X) ▼

X

8

*17 USC §506(e): Any person who knowingly makes a false representation of a material fact in the application for copyright registration provided for by section 409, or in any written statement filed in connection with the application, shall be fined not more than $2,500.

Form PA – Full   Rev: 07/2003   Print: 07/2003 — xx,000   Printed on recycled paper   U.S. Government Printing Office: 20xx-xxx/60,xxx

---

Figure 1.2 Form PA (Performing Arts) page 4.

Form SR

Detach and read these instructions before completing this form.
Make sure all applicable spaces have been filled in before you return this form.

When to Use This Form: Use Form SR for registration of published or unpublished sound recordings. It should be used when the copyright claim is limited to the sound recording itself, and it may also be used where the same copyright claimant is seeking simultaneous registration of the underlying musical, dramatic, or literary work embodied in the phonorecord.

With one exception, "sound recordings" are works that result from the fixation of a series of musical, spoken, or other sounds. The exception is for the audio portions of audiovisual works, such as a motion picture soundtrack or an audio cassette accompanying a filmstrip. These are considered a part of the audiovisual work as a whole.

Deposit to Accompany Application: An application for copyright registration must be accompanied by a deposit consisting of phonorecords representing the entire work for which registration is to be made.

Unpublished Work: Deposit one complete phonorecord.

Published Work: Deposit two complete phonorecords of the best edition, together with "any printed or other visually perceptible material" published with the phonorecords.

Work First Published Outside the United States: Deposit one complete phonorecord of the first foreign edition.

Contribution to a Collective Work: Deposit one complete phonorecord of the best edition of the collective work.

The Copyright Notice: Before March 1, 1989, the use of copyright notice was mandatory on all published works, and any work first published before that date should have carried a notice. For works first published on and after March 1, 1989, use of the copyright notice is optional. For more information about copyright notice, see Circular 3, *Copyright Notices.*

For Further Information: To speak to a Copyright Office staff member, call (202) 707-3000 (TTY: (202) 707-6737). Recorded information is available 24 hours a day. Order forms and other publications from Library of Congress, Copyright Office, 101 Independence Avenue SE, Washington, DC 20559-6000 or call the Forms and Publications Hotline at (202) 707-9100. Access and download circulars, forms, and other information from the Copyright Office website at *www.copyright.gov.*

PRIVACY ACT ADVISORY STATEMENT Required by the Privacy Act of 1974 (P.L. 93-579)
The authority for requesting this information is title 17 *USC*, secs. 409 and 410. Furnishing the requested information is voluntary. But if the information is not furnished, it may be necessary to delay or refuse registration and you may not be entitled to certain relief, remedies, and benefits provided in chapters 4 and 5 of title 17 *USC*.
The principal uses of the requested information are the establishment and maintenance of a public record and the examination of the application for compliance with the registration requirements of the copyright code.
Other routine uses include public inspection and copying, preparation of public indexes, preparation of public catalogs of copyright registrations, and preparation of search reports upon request.
NOTE: No other advisory statement will be given in connection with this application. Please keep this statement and refer to it if we communicate with you regarding this application.

Please type or print neatly using black ink. The form is used to produce the certificate.

 SPACE 1: Title

Title of This Work: Every work submitted for copyright registration must be given a title to identify that particular work. If the phonorecords or any accompanying printed material bears a title (or an identifying phrase that could serve as a title), transcribe that wording completely and exactly on the application. Indexing of the registration and future identification of the work may depend on the information you give here.

Previous, Alternative, or Contents Titles: Complete this space if there are any previous or alternative titles for the work under which someone searching for the registration might be likely to look, or under which a document pertaining to the work might be recorded. You may also give the individual contents titles, if any, in this space or you may use a Continuation Sheet. Circle the term that describes the titles given.

 SPACE 2: Author(s)

General Instructions: After reading these instructions, decide who are the "authors" of this work for copyright purposes. Then, unless the work is a "collective work," give the requested information about every "author" who contributed any appreciable amount of copyrightable matter to this version of the work. If you need further space, request additional Continuation Sheets. In the case of a collective work such as a collection of previously published or registered sound recordings, give information about the author of the collective work as a whole. If you are submitting this Form SR to cover the recorded musical, dramatic, or literary work as well as the sound recording itself, it is important for space 2 to include full information about the various authors of all of the material covered by the copyright claim, making clear the nature of each author's contribution.

Name of Author: The fullest form of the author's name should be given. Unless the work was "made for hire," the individual who actually created the work is its "author." In the case of a work made for hire, the statute provides that "the employer or other person for whom the work was prepared is considered the author."

What Is a "Work Made for Hire"? A "work made for hire" is defined as: (1) "a work prepared by an employee within the scope of his or her employment"; or (2) "a work specially ordered or commissioned for use as a contribution to a collective

work, as a part of a motion picture or other audiovisual work, as a translation, as a supplementary work, as a compilation, as an instructional text, as a test, as answer material for a test, or as an atlas, if the parties expressly agree in a written instrument signed by them that the work shall be considered a work made for hire." If you have checked "Yes" to indicate that the work was "made for hire," you must give the full legal name of the employer (or other person for whom the work was prepared). You may also include the name of the employee along with the name of the employer (for example: "Elster Record Co., employer for hire of John Ferguson").

"Anonymous" or "Pseudonymous" Work: An author's contribution to a work is "anonymous" if that author is not identified on the copies or phonorecords of the work. An author's contribution to a work is "pseudonymous" if that author is identified on the copies or phonorecords under a fictitious name. If the work is "anonymous" you may: (1) leave the line blank; or (2) state "anonymous" on the line; or (3) reveal the author's identity. If the work is "pseudonymous" you may: (1) leave the line blank; or (2) give the pseudonym and identify it as such (for example: "Huntley Haverstock, pseudonym"); or (3) reveal the author's name, making clear which is the real name and which is the pseudonym (for example: "Judith Barton, whose pseudonym is Madeline Elster"). However, the citizenship or domicile of the author *must* be given in all cases.

Dates of Birth and Death: If the author is dead, the statute requires that the year of death be included in the application unless the work is anonymous or pseudonymous. The author's birth date is optional, but is useful as a form of identification. Leave this space blank if the author's contribution was a "work made for hire."

Author's Nationality or Domicile: Give the country in which the author is a citizen, or the country in which the author is domiciled. Nationality or domicile *must* be given in all cases.

Nature of Authorship: Sound recording authorship is the performance, sound production, or both, that is fixed in the recording deposited for registration. Describe this authorship in space 2 as "sound recording." If the claim also covers the underlying work(s), include the appropriate authorship terms for each author, for example, "words," "music," "arrangement of music," or "text."

Generally, for the claim to cover both the sound recording and the underlying work(s), every author should have contributed to both the sound recording *and* the underlying work(s). If the claim includes artwork or photographs, include the appropriate term in the statement of authorship.

Figure 1.3 Form SR (Sound Recording) page 1.

SPACE 3: Creation and Publication

General Instructions: Do not confuse "creation" with "publication." Every application for copyright registration must state "the year in which creation of the work was completed." Give the date and nation of first publication only if the work has been published.

Creation: Under the statute, a work is "created" when it is fixed in a copy or phonorecord for the first time. Where a work has been prepared over a period of time, the part of the work existing in fixed form on a particular date constitutes the created work on that date. The date you give here should be the year in which the author completed the particular version for which registration is now being sought, even if other versions exist or if further changes or additions are planned.

Publication: The statute defines "publication" as "the distribution of copies or phonorecords of a work to the public by sale or other transfer of ownership, or by rental, lease, or lending"; a work is also "published" if there has been an "offering to distribute copies or phonorecords to a group of persons for purposes of further distribution, public performance, or public display." Give the full date (month, date, year) when, and the country where, publication first occurred. If first publication took place simultaneously in the United States and other countries, it is sufficient to state "U.S.A."

SPACE 4: Claimant(s)

Name(s) and Addresses(s) of Copyright Claimant(s): Give the name(s) and address(es) of the copyright claimant(s) in the work even if the claimant is the same as the author. Copyright in a work belongs initially to the author of the work (including, in the case of a work made for hire, the employer or other person for whom the work was prepared). The copyright claimant is either the author of the work or a person or organization to whom the copyright initially belonging to the author has been transferred.

Transfer: The statute provides that, if the copyright claimant is not the author, the application for registration must contain "a brief statement of how the claimant obtained ownership of the copyright." If any copyright claimant named in space 4a is not an author named in space 2, give a brief statement explaining how the claimant(s) obtained ownership of the copyright. Examples: "By written contract"; "Transfer of all rights by author"; "Assignment"; "By will." Do not attach transfer documents or other attachments or riders.

SPACE 5: Previous Registration

General Instructions: The questions in space 5 are intended to show whether an earlier registration has been made for this work and, if so, whether there is any basis for a new registration. As a rule, only one basic copyright registration can be made for the same version of a particular work.

Same Version: If this version is substantially the same as the work covered by a previous registration, a second registration is not generally possible unless: (1) the work has been registered in unpublished form and a second registration is now being sought to cover this first published edition; or (2) someone other than the author is copyright claimant in the earlier registration and the author is now seeking registration in his or her own name. If either of these two exceptions applies, check the appropriate box and give the earlier registration number and date. Otherwise, do not submit Form SR. Instead, write the Copyright Office for information about supplementary registration or recordation of transfers of copyright ownership.

Changed Version: If the work has been changed and you are now seeking reg-

istration to cover the additions or revisions, check the last box in space 5, give the earlier registration number and date, and complete both parts of space 6 in accordance with the instructions below.

Previous Registration Number and Date: If more than one previous registration has been made for the work, give the number and date of the latest registration.

SPACE 6: Derivative Work or Compilation

General Instructions: Complete space 6 if this work is a "changed version," "compilation," or "derivative work," and if it incorporates one or more earlier works that have already been published or registered for copyright, or that have fallen into the public domain, or sound recordings that were fixed before February 15, 1972. A "compilation" is defined as "a work formed by the collection and assembling of preexisting materials or of data that are selected, coordinated, or arranged in such a way that the resulting work as a whole constitutes an original work of authorship." A "derivative work" is "a work based on one or more preexisting works." Examples of derivative works include recordings reissued with substantial editorial revisions or abridgments of the recorded sounds, and recordings republished with new recorded material, or "any other form in which a work may be recast, transformed, or adapted." Derivative works also include works "consisting of editorial revisions, annotations, or other modifications" if these changes, as a whole, represent an original work of authorship.

Preexisting Material (space 6a): Complete this space *and* space 6b for derivative works. In this space identify the preexisting work that has been recast, transformed, or adapted. The preexisting work may be material that has been previously published, previously registered, or that is in the public domain. For example, the preexisting material might be: "1970 recording by Sperryville Symphony of Bach Double Concerto."

Material Added to This Work (space 6b): Give a brief, general statement of the additional new material covered by the copyright claim for which registration is sought. In the case of a derivative work, identify this new material. Examples: "Recorded performances on bands 1 and 3"; "Remixed sounds from original multitrack sound sources"; "New words, arrangement, and additional sounds." If the work is a compilation, give a brief, general statement describing both the material that has been compiled *and* the compilation itself. Example: "Compilation of 1938 Recordings by various swing bands."

SPACE 7, 8, 9: Fee, Correspondence, Certification, Return Address

Deposit Account: If you maintain a Deposit Account in the Copyright Office, identify it in space 7a. Otherwise, leave the space blank and send the filing fee with your application and deposit. (See space 8 on form.) (**Note:** Copyright Office fees are subject to change. For current fees, check the Copyright Office website at *www.copyright.gov*, write the Copyright Office, or call (202) 707-3000.)

Correspondence (space 7b): Give the name, address, area code, telephone number, fax number, and email address (if available) of the person to be consulted if correspondence about this application becomes necessary.

Certification (space 8): This application cannot be accepted unless it bears the date and the *handwritten signature* of the author or other copyright claimant, or of the owner of exclusive right(s), or of the duly authorized agent of the author, claimant, or owner of exclusive right(s).

Address for Return of Certificate (space 9): The address box must be completed legibly since the certificate will be returned in a window envelope.

MORE INFORMATION

"Works": "Works" are the basic subject matter of copyright; they are what authors create and copyright protects. The statute draws a sharp distinction between the "work" and "any material object in which the work is embodied."

"Copies" and "Phonorecords": These are the two types of material objects in which "works" are embodied. In general, "copies" are objects from which a work can be read or visually perceived, directly or with the aid of a machine or device, such as manuscripts, books, sheet music, film, and videotape. "Phonorecords" are objects embodying fixations of sounds, such as audio tapes and phonograph disks. For example, a song (the "work") can be reproduced in sheet music ("copies") or phonograph disks ("phonorecords"), or both.

"Sound Recordings": These are "works," not "copies" or "phonorecords." "Sound recordings" are "works that result from the fixation of a series of musical, spoken, or other sounds, but not including the sounds accompanying a motion picture or other audiovisual work." Example: When a record company issues a new release, the release will typically involve two distinct "works": the "musical work" that has been recorded, and the "sound recording" as a separate work in itself. The material objects that the record company sends out are "phonorecords": physical reproductions of both the "musical work" and the "sound recording."

Should You File More Than One Application? If your work consists of a recorded musical, dramatic, or literary work and if both that "work" and the sound recording as a separate "work" are eligible for registration, the application form you should file depends on the following:

File Only Form SR if: The copyright claimant is the same for both the musical, dramatic, or literary work and for the sound recording, and you are seeking a single registration to cover both of these "works."

File Only Form PA (or Form TX) if: You are seeking to register only the musical, dramatic, or literary work, not the sound recording. Form PA is appropriate for works of the performing arts; Form TX is for nondramatic literary works.

Separate Applications Should Be Filed on Form PA (or Form TX) and on Form SR if: (1) The copyright claimant for the musical, dramatic, or literary work is different from the copyright claimant for the sound recording; or (2) You prefer to have separate registrations for the musical, dramatic, or literary work and for the sound recording.

Figure 1.3 Form SR (Sound Recording) page 2.

For best results, fill in the form on-screen and then print it.

Form SR
For a Sound Recording
UNITED STATES COPYRIGHT OFFICE

REGISTRATION NUMBER

SR   SRU
EFFECTIVE DATE OF REGISTRATION

Month   Day   Year

DO NOT WRITE ABOVE THIS LINE. IF YOU NEED MORE SPACE, USE A SEPARATE CONTINUATION SHEET.

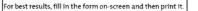

1

TITLE OF THIS WORK ▼

PREVIOUS, ALTERNATIVE, OR CONTENTS TITLES (CIRCLE ONE) ▼

2 a

NAME OF AUTHOR ▼

DATES OF BIRTH AND DEATH
Year Born ▼   Year Died ▼

Was this contribution to the work a "work made for hire"?
❏ Yes
❏ No

AUTHOR'S NATIONALITY OR DOMICILE
Name of Country
OR { Citizen of ▶
{ Domiciled in ▶

WAS THIS AUTHOR'S CONTRIBUTION TO THE WORK
Anonymous?   ❏ Yes ❏ No
Pseudonymous?   ❏ Yes ❏ No

If the answer to either of these questions is "Yes," see detailed instructions.

NATURE OF AUTHORSHIP Briefly describe nature of material created by this author in which copyright is claimed. ▼

NOTE

Under the law, the "author" of a "work made for hire" is generally the employer, not the employee (see instructions). For any part of this work that was "made for hire," check "Yes" in the space provided, give the employer (or other person for whom the work was prepared) as "Author" of that part, and leave the space for dates of birth and death blank

b

NAME OF AUTHOR ▼

DATES OF BIRTH AND DEATH
Year Born ▼   Year Died ▼

Was this contribution to the work a "work made for hire"?
❏ Yes
❏ No

AUTHOR'S NATIONALITY OR DOMICILE
Name of Country
OR { Citizen of ▶
{ Domiciled in ▶

WAS THIS AUTHOR'S CONTRIBUTION TO THE WORK
Anonymous?   ❏ Yes ❏ No
Pseudonymous?   ❏ Yes ❏ No

If the answer to either of these questions is "Yes," see detailed instructions.

NATURE OF AUTHORSHIP Briefly describe nature of material created by this author in which copyright is claimed. ▼

c

NAME OF AUTHOR ▼

DATES OF BIRTH AND DEATH
Year Born ▼   Year Died ▼

Was this contribution to the work a "work made for hire"?
❏ Yes
❏ No

AUTHOR'S NATIONALITY OR DOMICILE
Name of Country
OR { Citizen of ▶
{ Domiciled in ▶

WAS THIS AUTHOR'S CONTRIBUTION TO THE WORK
Anonymous?   ❏ Yes ❏ No
Pseudonymous?   ❏ Yes ❏ No

If the answer to either of these questions is "Yes," see detailed instructions.

NATURE OF AUTHORSHIP Briefly describe nature of material created by this author in which copyright is claimed. ▼

3 a

YEAR IN WHICH CREATION OF THIS WORK WAS COMPLETED

◀ Year This information must be given in all cases.

b DATE AND NATION OF FIRST PUBLICATION OF THIS PARTICULAR WORK
Complete this information ONLY if this work has been published.
Month ▶   Day ▶   Year ▶   ◀ Nation

4 a

See instructions before completing this space

COPYRIGHT CLAIMANT(S) Name and address must be given even if the claimant is the same as the author given in space 2. ▼

b TRANSFER If the claimant(s) named here in space 4 is (are) different from the author(s) named in space 2, give a brief statement of how the claimant(s) obtained ownership of the copyright. ▼

DO NOT WRITE HERE OFFICE USE ONLY

APPLICATION RECEIVED

ONE DEPOSIT RECEIVED

TWO DEPOSITS RECEIVED

FUNDS RECEIVED

MORE ON BACK ▶ • Complete all applicable spaces (numbers 5-9) on the reverse side of this page.
• See detailed instructions.   • Sign the form at line 8.

DO NOT WRITE HERE
Page 1 of _____ pages

Figure 1.3 Form SR (Sound Recording) page 3.

DO NOT WRITE ABOVE THIS LINE. IF YOU NEED MORE SPACE, USE A SEPARATE CONTINUATION SHEET.

PREVIOUS REGISTRATION Has registration for this work, or for an earlier version of this work, already been made in the Copyright Office?

❏ Yes ❏ No If your answer is "Yes," why is another registration being sought? (Check appropriate box) ▼

a. ❏ This work was previously registered in unpublished form and now has been published for the first time.

b. ❏ This is the first application submitted by this author as copyright claimant.

c. ❏ This is a changed version of the work, as shown by space 6 on this application.

If your answer is "Yes," give: **Previous Registration Number** ▼   **Year of Registration** ▼

5

DERIVATIVE WORK OR COMPILATION

a **Preexisting Material** Identify any preexisting work or works that this work is based on or incorporates. ▼

b **Material Added to This Work** Give a brief, general statement of the material that has been added to this work and in which copyright is claimed. ▼

6

See instructions
before completing
this space.

DEPOSIT ACCOUNT If the registration fee is to be charged to a deposit account established in the Copyright Office, give name and number of Account.

a Name ▼   Account Number ▼

b **CORRESPONDENCE** Give name and address to which correspondence about this application should be sent. Name/Address/Apt/City/State/Zip ▼

Area code and daytime telephone number   Fax number

Email

7

CERTIFICATION* I, the undersigned, hereby certify that I am the

Check only one ▼

❏ author

❏ other copyright claimant

❏ owner of exclusive right(s)

❏ authorized agent of

Name of author or other copyright claimant, or owner of exclusive right(s) ▲

of the work identified in this application and that the statements made by me in this application are correct to the best of my knowledge.

Typed or printed name and date ▼ If this application gives a date of publication in space 3, do not sign and submit it before that date.

Date

Handwritten signature ▼

8

Certificate will be mailed in window envelope to this address	Name ▼
	Number/Street/Apt ▼
	City/State/Zip ▼

YOU MUST:
• Complete all necessary spaces
• Sign your application in space 8

**SEND ALL 3 ELEMENTS
IN THE SAME PACKAGE:**
1. Application form
2. Nonrefundable filing fee in check or money order payable to *Register of Copyrights*
3. Deposit material

MAIL TO:
Library of Congress
Copyright Office
101 Independence Avenue SE
Washington, DC 20559-6000

9

*17 USC §506(e): Any person who knowingly makes a false representation of a material fact in the application for copyright registration provided for by section 409, or in any written statement filed in connection with the application, shall be fined not more than $2,500.

Form SR-Full Rev: 11/2006 Print: 11/2006— 60,000 Printed on recycled paper   U.S. Government Printing Office: 2007-330-945/60,138

Figure 1.3 Form SR (Sound Recording) page 4.

MYTH-BUSTER: The Oklahoma, or Poor Man's Copyright

A myth that circulates widely in the songwriting community is that a songwriter can protect his work without paying any fee to the copyright office, simply by mailing a copy of the song to himself with a return receipt requested, and keeping the package unopened. Although we have seen books that maintain that this procedure may hold up in Britain, there is no evidence that this process will work in the United States. In addition to the rights and safeguards previously explained, registering a copyright with the U.S. Copyright Office also enables the publisher and/or songwriter to receive statutory damages and attorneys' fees if a lawsuit proves to be successful. Contrary to urban myth, the so-called Poor Man's Copyright provides very little in the way of technical protections for your works.

Copyright notice

Use of a copyright notice—consisting of the letter C inside of a circle ("©"), or the word "Copyright," followed by the year of the first publication of the work and the name of the copyright holder—was part of previous United States statutory requirements. But in 1989, the United States enacted the Berne Convention Implementation Act, amending the 1976 Copyright Act to conform to most of the provisions of the Berne Convention. As a result, the use of copyright notices has become optional to claim copyright, because the Berne Convention makes copyright automatic. However, notice of copyright does have consequences in terms of allowable damages in an infringement lawsuit in some places.

The phrase "All Rights Reserved" was once a necessary formal notice that all rights granted under existing copyright law are retained by the copyright holder and that legal action may be taken against copyright infringement.

Duration of copyright

The duration of copyright has changed several times as Congress refined compromises over the law. In 1998 the United States passed the Sonny Bono Act to extend copyright protection from fifty to seventy years after the death of the last surviving author. Prior to the Sonny Bono twenty year copyright term extension, copyright protection for works registered before January 1, 1978 was seventy-five years. The current duration of copyright protection for published works is as follows:

- Works registered before January 1, 1923: copyright protection for seventy-five years has expired, and these works (registered in 1922 or earlier) entered the public domain on January 1, 1998.
- Works created after January 1, 1978: life of the longest surviving author, plus seventy years.

Copyright protection outside the United States is determined by the laws of the country where you wish to use a work. Copyright protection may be ninety-five years from publication date, fifty to seventy years after the death of the last surviving author, or other criteria depending on where the work was first published and how the work is to be used. Limits and Exceptions to Copyright are discussed in Chapter 12.

2 Sources of income, royalties, and licenses

The business of music publishing encompasses the entire area of administering and exploiting musical works. Although this book provides clarification of the role that music publishing plays within the nearly $30 billion generated worldwide each year in the music industry as a whole, we will see that the myriad copyright laws, the international marketplace for music, the evolving digital distribution arena, and the enormous amount of music that is consumed—bought, broadcast, licensed, and downloaded throughout the world—creates a staggering array of monitoring, accounting, and collection issues for both the creators and the users of music. In this chapter we will discuss the sources of income available to a composer and music publisher, and we will also provide information about the way that these revenues are generated.

Sources of income

Lawyers call it the Copyright Act. Songwriters and publishers call it Sources of Income. Each of the five basic copyright provisions establishes a royalty structure for the benefit of the songwriter and publisher. Consider, as well, that each of these income streams can generate royalties not only in the United States, but in nearly every foreign territory in the world. The complexities of collecting these royalties, however, demands that creators understand the basic principles of royalty collection—and hire professionals that have expertise in domestic and foreign royalty collections. Composers and songwriters can earn royalties from many sources including record, CD, and tape sales (mechanicals), U.S. and foreign television, cable and radio performances, theater performances, downloads, streaming, and artist and record producer royalties, among others.

● The song: the center of gravity

The multi-billion dollar music industry—CDs, film scores, radio performance, digital downloads, sheet music, live concerts, Broadway musicals, and theme songs—revolves around the song. Record companies, publishing companies, artist management companies, talent agencies, entertainment lawyers, and even the iPod, all thrive on the power and magnetism of a song. When performed by the right artist or band, a single song can catapult a career, can generate millions of dollars in royalties, and can sustain entire companies. The following chapters outline how the art of a songwriter or composer, when coupled with the expertise of a music publisher, can create the nucleus of a virtually unlimited source of income.

The major sources of royalties for composers and publishers is generated through music performed on radio and television ("performance income"), music placed in film and television programs ("synchronization income"), record/CD sales ("mechanical income"), and numerous ancillary sources of income, including sheet music sales, advertising campaigns, Internet transmissions, Grand (theatrical) Rights, and new media (video games, ringtones, etc.).

Performing rights: music played on radio, television, and in public establishments

Approximately 50 to 75 percent of a songwriter's compensation can come from performance royalties, primarily through radio and television broadcasts. Performance royalties are payable to the writer and publisher whenever the film or television program is performed, picked up in a performance rights survey, and when a song is monitored on a radio performance. A crossover hit song, particularly one that is a hit single and is the centerpiece of a hit album, can generate as much as half a million dollars, split between the publisher and songwriter, in a single year. Over the cumulative course of several years, a major number one song can generate nearly one million dollars in combined writer and publisher distributions, and a successful TV-series theme song can generate numbers in excess of one million dollars. The factors that affect the level of performance royalties include: the number of radio stations playing the song and the number of weeks or months that the song remains popular, the frequency with which the composition or score is used on television broadcasts, how the song is used in a production (background, visual vocal, network broadcast, or smaller cable exhibition), and whether the song is receiving foreign exposure and performances.

Synchronization rights: music embedded in film or television productions

A synchronization license is issued by a copyright owner, to a producer, granting the right to synchronize the musical composition in timed relation with audio-visual images on film or videotape. The producer of the audiovisual production (television show, film, video game, commercial) requests a "synch license" from the song publisher. "Synch fees" can generate substantial income, which typically range between $500.00 and $10,000.00 for a placement in a television production, $10,000.00 and $40,000.00 for a placement in a film, and more than $35,000.00 for use in a national commercial. These rights are negotiated, licensed, and administered by the publisher, who accounts directly to the writer(s) for her half of the fees. More about synch rights in Chapter 7.

Mechanical rights: royalties generated from record sales and downloads

A mechanical royalty is earned for any "phonorecord" (including CDs, tapes, vinyl, and digital downloads) that is manufactured and distributed with a copyrighted song on it. A mechanical license is written permission from the publisher to manufacture and distribute a record, CD, or audio tape for a specific copyrighted composition. Once a song has been publicly distributed, any person may obtain a "compulsory" mechanical license, as provided for by law (U.S. Code 17, section 115) by complying with the statutory procedures, one of which is paying the 2007 "statutory mechanical rate" of 9.1 cents per song, multiplied by the number of songs manufactured and distributed (rate × units). Originally named for the earliest mechanical formats of record production, the mechanical royalty rate has become a significant source of income for those writers and publishers who sell a lot of records.

Licenses, assignments, and transfers of rights

Ownership in copyright also includes the option of granting exclusive licenses, transfers, or assignments of rights from one party to another. Exclusive licenses, to be effective, must be granted in a written instrument signed by the grantor. No special form of transfer or grant is required. A simple document that identifies the work involved and the rights being granted is sufficient. Non-exclusive grants (non-exclusive licenses) need not be in writing under U.S. law. They can be oral or even implied by the behavior of the parties. Transfers of copyright ownership, including exclusive licenses, should be registered and recorded in the U.S. Copyright Office. While registering is not required to make the grant effective, as we have seen, registration does offer important benefits.

For example, an artist who records an album will often sign an agreement with a record company in which the musician agrees to transfer all copyright in the recordings in exchange for royalties and other considerations. The creator (and original copyright holder) benefits, or expects to, from production and marketing capabilities far beyond those of the author. Songwriters and composers similarly enter agreements with publishers in exchange for monetary advances or services. In the digital age of music, music may be copied and distributed at minimal cost through the Internet, however the record industry attempts to provide promotion and marketing for the artist and his work so it can reach a much larger audience. A copyright holder need not transfer all rights completely. Some of the rights may be transferred, or else the copyright holder may grant another party a non-exclusive license to copy and/or distribute the work in a particular region or for a specified period of time.

Mechanical license fees and the Harry Fox Agency

The mechanical license is the agreement whereby a music publisher grants a license to a record company to record and sell copies of a composition, and pay a license fee—the mechanical royalty—to the publisher, for every record sold that embodies their composition. The publisher retains the right to control the first recording of a song, but once that recording is released, anyone could record the song, as long as it was licensed, and royalties were paid. Under this license, anyone who wishes to copy a work covered by the law does not need to obtain the permission of the copyright holder, but instead, simply files the proper notice and pays a set fee established by statute for every copy made. At this writing (2007), the fee is 9.1 cents per song sold or 1.75 cents per minute of music, whichever fee is greater. The math tells a very clear story: at 9.1 cents per manufactured song, a million-selling single would generate $91,000.00 in mechanical royalties, which would be split 50 percent to the writer(s) share, and 50 percent to the publisher(s) share. If a writer or publisher had several songs on one CD, the mechanical royalty (rate × units) would be multiplied by the number of songs included on that CD. For the copyright owner(s) who had ten songs on a million-selling CD, the mechanical income would be $91,000.00/song × 10, or $910,000.00!

The Harry Fox Agency (HFA) is an organization that collects mechanical royalties for music publishers in the United States. For a fee of 6.75 percent of the royalties collected, HFA issues mechanical licenses to record companies on behalf of their publisher members. Over twenty-seven thousand publishers use HFA, because it frees them from the paperwork burden of issuing licenses, and the organization is a subsidiary of the National Music Publishers Association. HFA will also issue digital licenses, and pursue record company audits, if royalties are not paid. HFA also represents American publishers in foreign sub-publishing deals in the collection of royalties.

Some small publishers elect to save the fees and to negotiate licenses on their own. For larger publishers, the fee is often regarded as well worth abandoning the challenges of domestic and international royalty collections.

An artist who is making an album in small quantities can go online and license a song from HFA in a pressing as small as 500 copies. In that instance, artists will pre-pay HFA the mechanical license fees. The HFA office is not involved in synchronization licenses, because these fees are entirely negotiable, and structured on a case-by-case basis.

Controlled-composition clause

"Controlled compositions" are those songs designated in the provisions of a recording agreement, whereby the artist, who is also the composer of compositions recorded under that agreement, agrees to license those compositions to the record company at a reduced mechanical royalty rate, usually ¾ (75 percent) of the otherwise applicable Statutory Rate. The controlled composition clause, therefore, limits the amount of mechanical royalties the record company is required to pay for the records it releases, and holds the artist responsible for reimbursing the excess payments of mechanical royalties, if any, over a specified limit. In essence, the record companies are compelling writer-artists to subsidize the payment of mechanical royalties.

The Copyright Office sets the statutory rate for mechanical royalties, increasing every two years according to changes in cost of living as determined by the Consumer Price Index. The rate increases are by authority of the 1976 amendment to the Copyright Act. The first rate increase was in 1981. It was at about this time that the Controlled Composition clause became commonplace in record contracts. The controlled songs are locked in at a reduced rate that will never increase, preventing statutory cost of living increases. Under the compulsory license provisions of the Copyright Act, record labels are also required to pay mechanical royalties on all records "made and distributed." Record labels avoid complying with this provision of the law by refusing to pay for so-called "free goods." This confusing term "free goods" is not defined as promo albums. Rather, many major labels define "free goods" as 15 percent of the records they sell. Using this provision, major labels calculate royalties on only 85 percent of records sold.

The definition of "controlled composition" casts a wide net, including songs written by producers on the record. Customarily, the record company hires producers without negotiating a reduced mechanical royalty rate for the songs that they write for the record. The artist is forced, therefore, to make up the difference. Generally regarded by songwriters as one of the most onerous clauses in a recording agreement, the main purpose of the controlled composition clause is to allow record companies to avoid paying writers and publishers the full statutory mechanical license rate, thereby thwarting copyright law royalty rates.

Songs used on medium- or low-priced albums, or by record clubs, are also often paid at rates lower than the prevailing mechanical rates. The record company reasoning behind these reduced rates is that since there is less profit on lower-priced albums, the artist and the music publisher and songwriter should, therefore, be willing to accept a lower royalty.

3 Performing rights

The performing right

With nearly $2 billion collected annually for songwriters and publishers throughout the world for the "public performance" of their works, "performance rights" royalties have become one of the most lucrative sources of publishing royalties. For many writers and publishers, the performance rights royalties are their largest source of income. In the United States, the primary source of performance income is generated by music "performed"—played—on radio and television. Significant additional performance income is generated by music performed (live or recorded) in nightclubs, hotels, and retail establishments which use music in an effort to enhance their business. The U.S. Copyright Law, which has recognized the Performing Right of songwriters, composers, and publishers since 1897, is similar to other copyright and patent protections. The law was designed to encourage artists to create musical works, by protecting the integrity of the work, and entitling the creator to be compensated for the use of her work in public by the entity which benefits from playing the music.

Performing Rights Organizations

As there are literally thousands of individual broadcasters, bars, nightclubs, hotels, and other entities who "publicly perform" copyrighted works, it would be virtually impossible for individual songwriters to monitor all of the potential domestic (and global) music uses and users of their works. Because of the obvious challenges in managing royalty payments for music uses, Performing Rights Organizations (PROs) have been formed to license music users, monitor music uses, and collect royalties for hundreds of thousands of works. The PRO collects license fees on behalf of writers and publishers from businesses which use their music, making the licensing process easier. This method allows thousands of music users to work with thousands of music creators through one of the licensing organizations. In the United States, the three Performing Rights Organizations—ASCAP (American Society of Composers, Authors, and Publishers), BMI (Broadcast Music Incorporated), and SESAC (Society of European Stage Authors and Composers)—issue blanket licenses and collect fees from music "users," on behalf of their affiliated writers and publishers, for the collection of their non-dramatic ("small rights") public performance royalties. The rights to perform music in Broadway-type theatrical shows—known as "grand rights"—are not represented by the PROs, and must be obtained directly from the publisher of the music.

PROs, therefore, acquire non-exclusive rights from writer and publisher affiliates, and in turn, grant Public Performance Licenses (PPLs) to use their entire repertories to users of music. Although the overwhelming majority of all composers choose to be represented by one of the PROs, the unique non-exclusive characteristic of U.S. performance rights operation does allow for writers and publishers to enter into direct licenses with broadcasters for the payment of their performance rights royalties. In direct license situations, writers and publishers choose to negotiate directly with the broadcaster of their music, and effectively remove the PRO from the royalty process for that specific license. Direct license deals are only applicable to U.S. payments of performance income. Although direct licenses may be appropriate in some rare circumstances, writers and publishers are strongly encouraged to seek the advice of their PRO before entering into any direct license.

PROs collect license fees from each user of music that obtains a Public Performance License, and distributes to its writers and publishers all the money collected, after deducting operating expenses for the organization. Every composer is free to select any one of the three PROs to collect her performance income. The choice of which PRO to select is entirely free, voluntary, and personal to each composer. Some of the distinctions between the three PROs are discussed below. Once a composer has selected a PRO, the publishing portion of that writer's works must be registered with the same PRO as that of the composer. To reiterate, the PRO affiliation of the publishing portion of every song must reside with the same Performing Rights Organization as that of the writer of that work.

> Unlike the payment of all other music royalties, writers and publishers, separately, enter into agreements with a Performing Rights Organization of their choice, granting permission to license performances of their works. Performing rights income is paid separately and directly to both the publisher and the songwriter. The writer does not receive this income from the publisher, as is true of all other sources of publishing revenue. Performance rights income is earned and distributed separately for the writer's half and the publisher's half, and, therefore, this is the only royalty income that is paid directly to the writer for her share of the song, and paid directly to the publisher for her share of the song. All other royalties are paid 100 percent to the publisher . . . with the publisher responsible for accounting to, and distributing, the writer's share back to the writer.

There are nominal processing fees to apply for BMI or ASCAP membership, and qualified applicants can join as a writer member or a publisher member, or both. The minimum ASCAP writer membership term is one year, while the minimum BMI contract term is two years. It is not possible to be a writer member of two organizations at the same time. It is possible, however, to leave one organization and affiliate with another PRO, but only after the term of the original membership agreement has terminated. The songs that were written during the term of membership with one PRO generally remain under royalty collection with that organization, even if the writer moves to another PRO. Although it is possible to move works from one society to another, the rules for moving song catalogues are detailed, and are tied to the term of "radio licenses in effect." Transfers of catalogues to another society, therefore, are complicated and require the coordination and approval of the relinquishing society. Performing rights have become increasingly lucrative, with ASCAP and BMI each collecting gross receipts of over $700 million in 2006. The revenues of SESAC are not available to the public, because the organization is privately owned, although they have been estimated at $30 to $50 million a year. Although songwriters can affiliate with only one of the performing rights groups at any one time, they are free to co-write with members of the other organizations. Most major music publishers, however, operate a publishing entity under each of the three performing rights organizations, in order to accommodate the requirement that a publisher's PRO affiliation must mirror the PRO affiliation of its writer.

Title Registrations: the roadmap to performance royalties

In order to receive royalty income from song performances, it is critical that all publishers and songwriters submit Title Registrations of each of their recorded and released songs to their chosen Performing Rights Organization. All of the organizations have websites which enable their writer and publisher members to register their songs online. If you are a songwriter, do not assume that your publisher has registered your song. Remember that performance rights are paid separately and directly to the publisher, and to the songwriter. If your song is not registered, you will not receive payment for it. If you have to correct the fact that your songs had not been registered, it will create delays in the payment process, and you may lose some of the income that should have been received.

In writing music for film or television, make certain that a "cue sheet" has been prepared by the production company, and submitted and registered with the Performing Rights Organization. Royalty payments are dependent on how and when the music was used on a program, and can only be accounted for through the evaluation of a cue sheet. More on cue sheets later in this chapter.

REALWORLD: "Be careful what you ask for"

It's common knowledge, within the music industry, that "owning the publishing" is a good thing. Unfortunately, the business and practice of owning the publishing is much more difficult than the theory. Songwriters and record companies each seek to own or retain some of the publishing rights of the songs that they are involved with. It is not unusual, therefore, for some record companies to offer an artist a recording contract coupled with a "publishing contract." Problems can arise, however, when an over-zealous—and under-educated—record company does, indeed, acquire publishing rights in their artists' songs, but fails to properly execute the song registration processes. During the height of its recent success, a very prominent independent record label had the clout to seek and acquire publishing rights whenever a writer-artist was signed to its label. The record company was enjoying great success, and its focus was on breaking new artists, and promoting their record sales. So far, so good. The record company Business Affairs folks were certainly educated in drafting recording agreements, and they were certainly aware that they should "own the publishing to their artists' songs," where possible. But there is much more to owning and managing the publishing rights than simply entering into a publishing agreement. The record company, over a period of several years, did acquire the publishing rights to their artists' very popular songs. The record company did not, however, employ knowledgeable publishing administrators or executives. Although the publishing contracts were signed, the label never registered the titles with a Performing Rights Organization. Notwithstanding the enormous sales success of the records, the radio airplay performance income for the label-publisher (and songwriters) was never realized or received, because the PRO was never supplied with Title Registrations. The error was undetected for more than four years, and the loss of performance rights income was substantial.

Song performances, identification, and music surveys

Given that there are literally millions of songs performed every year in the United States—in thousands of broadcast and retail environments—it is currently impossible to monitor and survey each of these music performances. Technological advances in digital song "fingerprinting," watermarking, and data identification procedures, however, may soon make it feasible to accurately identify all broadcast and transmitted musical works. Although each of the PROs utilize some digital identification technologies, until these tools are fully implemented, all of the Performing Rights Organizations must rely on various sampling procedures to monitor music uses. Utilizing monitoring and survey systems, such as BDS (Broadcast Data System) scans, program playlists, broadcast logs, and scientifically designed sample surveys, PROs attempt to determine how often a song is performed, and then distribute the collected license fees to writers and publishers based on how often a song is detected in the survey. BMI combines census and sample radio airplay data totaling more than 4,000,000 hours, providing a wide-ranging picture of radio airplay. BMI's analysis of TV music is drawn from a survey of more than 15,000,000 broadcast hours per year.

Using a combination of the existing monitoring services, PROs are able to calculate and project the approximate number of total public performances for songs, cues, and scores for member writers and publishers. Through this sampling process, PROs attempt to accurately track and monitor the works of popular and lesser-known songwriters and composers, and compensate them for the use of their local public performances.

Although the three U.S. PROs have the same mission—to collect and distribute Public Performance License royalties—each of these organizations has unique rules, regulations, and widely different methods of valuing and distributing royalties to their writer and publisher members. Co-author Dick Weissman is a composer of folk-based instrumental music, and he has been a member of both BMI and ASCAP at different times. In the case of both of these performing rights groups, the royalties he has received for U.S. airplay have been minute. On the other hand, he has received relatively generous royalty checks for airplay in England, Canada, Belgium, Japan, and several other European countries. This is because radio is largely government-operated in these countries, and a larger percentage of music played on the radio gets surveyed and monitored. His experiences in this regard, along with the experiences of many who write or publish music in the areas of blues, bluegrass, folk music, and world music styles, cast doubt on societies' contentions that eventually all writers' and publishers' share of broadcast royalties will, as they often maintain, "even out." All network television broadcasts are now monitored, and so the compensation given to publishers and songwriters in this medium is much more equitable. As survey techniques continue to improve and become more comprehensive, an increasing number of cable stations are also being monitored on a complete basis. Although the monitoring and survey techniques of radio and television stations vary among the three PROs, they each utilize fundamentally similar methodologies to identify what and how much music is being performed publicly. Royalties are distributed to writer and publisher members, on a quarterly basis, as a result of the song usage information that they can identify from their licensees. The following are key sources of performance data and income:

Radio—PROs monitor thousands of hours of radio performances and playlists each year, and license all commercial radio stations in the United States. Each quarter, PROs ask a diverse segment of these stations to submit song performance data for the period. Using these results, together with census data from hundreds of the highest license-fee-paying radio stations and performance data from the sample data system, PROs are then able to calculate and project an approximate number of total public performances of their member writers' and publishers' works.

Television—Much like the radio survey, PROs rely on the services of data gathering companies, which supply performance information on television shows broadcast on network, cable, and local television carriers. PROs now conduct census surveys—complete minute-by-minute song histories—of music broadcast on network and most major cable television stations. The production companies that produce the programs are required to supply the PROs with a cue sheet—the comprehensive list of the music performed in each show. Generally prepared by the music editor, the cue sheet lists the titles, chronologically, of all music contained in a production, together with the writers, the publishers, and their applicable performance rights society, how the music was used, and the duration of the use. More on cue sheets in Chapter 7. Music used in commercials, infomercials, and advertising campaigns also can generate substantial royalties.

Film—PROs credit the appropriate writer and publisher of music included in a film, according to the information contained on the film cue sheet. PROs monitor films performed on television in the United States, but due to a technical court ruling, music in film is exempt from generating royalties when shown in U.S. movie theaters.

U.S. movie theater exemption

A significant exemption to the collection of performance income in the United States comes as a result of the so-called "Alden-Rochelle" lawsuit. At the time of the suit, movie studios also owned the theaters their films were shown in. Challenges were made concerning the performance rights fees that were being charged at the theaters. The result of the suit was the creation of an exemption for movie theaters in the United States from paying public performance royalties to the three PROs for music contained in the films they exhibited in their theaters. Songs and musical scores shown in U.S. movie theaters, therefore, do not generate performance royalties for their publishers or writers. Music in movies shown in *foreign* territories, on the other hand, is surveyed and can generate substantial income for songwriters, composers, and publishers. Performance income in foreign territories is based on local box office receipts generated by the film. Foreign public performances, whether on radio or in film or television, can generate substantial additional performance rights income. Foreign royalties are discussed in Chapter 10.

Other significant sources of public performance royalties include live concert venues, commercial music services (Muzak, DMX, AEI, Music Choice, etc.), new media (websites, ringtone providers, digital jukeboxes, etc.), music-on-hold in businesses, and music performed in nightclubs, concerts, hotels, and retail establishments.

Cue sheets

Much like the Title Registration for songs, the cue sheet is the cornerstone of all royalty payments for music used in film and television productions. After a motion picture/television program has been produced and a final version has been edited for release or distribution, the production company will prepare a music cue sheet (see Figure 3.1). The cue sheet is a log of all the music used in a production. This information includes: Series/Film Title,

Sample Music Cue Sheet

Series/Film Title: *When I Grow Up*
Episode Title/Number: *"Rock Star" - Ep #101*
Estimated Airdate: *1-22-07*
Program Length: *60 Minutes*
Program Type: *Comedy series*

Company Name: *NSM Productions*
Address: *1234 Stardom's Door, Hollywood*
Phone: *1-800-777-7777*
Contact: *Music Supervisor*
Network Station: *NSM Network*

Cue #	Cue Title	Use *	Timing	Composer(s) Affiliation/%	Publisher(s) Affiliation/%
1	When I Grow Up Theme	MT	0:14	Daniel Alan Kirkpatrick (ASCAP) 75% William A. Salisbury (ASCAP) 12.5% Earl L. Serrato (ASCAP) 12.5%	Bluesmaster Music (ASCAP) 50% North Port Music (ASCAP) 50%
2	Allnighter	VI	0:08	Kenneth Burgomaster (ASCAP) 100%	North Port Music (ASCAP) 50% Kenneth Burgomaster (ASCAP) 50%
3	Five Four	V V	0:12	Mariana Bernoski (BMI) 33.34% Willow Williamson (ASCAP) 33.33% Christina Agamanolis (ASCAP) 33.33%	Mariana Bernoski (BMI) 16.67% Willow Williamson (ASCAP) 16.67% Sonic Still Publishing (ASCAP) 16.67% North Port Music (ASCAP) 33.33% Three Degrees Music (BMI) 16.67%
4	You Can Rock & Roll	BV	1:03	Robert Harlow (ASCAP) 50% John Krautner (ASCAP) 50%	North Port Music (ASCAP) 25% Rhythm King Music (PRS) 50% Peacock Angel (ASCAP) 25%
5	I Wanna Be	ET	0:11	Lisa Campai (ASCAP) 100%	LoveSloger Music (ASCAP) 50% North Port Music (ASCAP) 50%

* USE CODES: **MT** = Main Title **VI** = Visual Instrumental **BV** = Background Vocal
V V = Visual Vocal **ET** = End Title **BI** = Background Instrumental
T = Theme

Figure 3.1 Music cue sheet.

Episode Title, Air Date, Production Company Information, Song/ Cue Title, Composer, Publisher, Performing Rights Organization, Timing, and Usage. If there is more than one composer for an individual piece of music, or if the writer and publisher split their royalties on other than a 50/50 basis, this must also be indicated on the cue sheet.

Since Performing Rights Organizations and other representatives of rights holders use music cue sheets to determine how music was used in a production, and how to calculate the royalty payments that are to be made when a film or television show is exhibited, it is essential that a cue sheet be completed accurately. With the increase in independent producers and cable operations, the filing of accurate cue sheets has become even more crucial to tracking the use of music in film and television productions. These newcomers to the industry are sometimes unfamiliar with, or unaware of, the legal and professional responsibilities involved in using the music of composers and publishers whose rights are represented by performing rights societies. By reviewing a copy of the cue sheet, the writer and publisher can correct any inaccuracies before the producer distributes the cue sheet to performing right and other organizations throughout the world.

Income from radio play

Each of the three Performing Rights Organizations has varying criteria that determine compensation generated from radio airplay. Principal among these are frequency of the song's airplay, and the gross advertising income of the station playing the song. A radio station's Public Performance License fee is based upon a calculated percentage of its gross advertising revenues; therefore a very popular, highly rated station receives considerably more advertising revenue than does a smaller market station, and therefore pays considerably more in license fees than does the smaller station. College and Public radio stations, which receive relatively little in the way of advertising revenues, consequently generate very little in the way of Public Performance License revenues. Songs airing on the highly rated, high-income stations clearly generate more performance income than do songs which enjoy airplay occurring primarily on small market stations. Radio royalties provide one of the single largest sources of performance income for writers and publishers, and cross-over hits, which appear on industry trade charts and magazines in more than one musical genre, provide the largest source of radio income. If a song appears on several of these charts at the same time, it is quite literally being played by hundreds of radio stations at any given moment, generating significant performance income. A popular song in a limited genre, such as bluegrass, may be in heavy rotation, but this may be occurring on only a few dozen radio stations throughout the country, or on programs that are only broadcast a few hours each week. These limited-genre songs may not show up in sample surveys as often as more broadly performed songs, and therefore their royalties are smaller than songs played in more numerous markets. A simple maxim for airplay royalties: "the more a song is played . . . the more a song is paid." A Top Five pop song on the charts can often generate more than $200,000.00 in performance income for the writer, and more than $200,000.00 in performance income for the publisher.

Income from television

Although performance royalties from television uses can be very lucrative, the process of identifying and valuing those performances is fairly complex. Several factors influence the value of music used in television: the type of use of the music (background, vocal, theme, etc.), the time of day that the music is performed (afternoons, prime time, overnight), and the duration of the song performed, and so on. Network and syndicated television shows also generate more royalties than do local shows, primarily because they are being broadcast to a much wider audience. Performance income from television is more fully discussed in Chapter 7.

Performing rights and live performances

Prior to the 1990s, neither publishers nor songwriters received much in the way of royalties for the music used in live performances. In recent years, the two largest societies have started to monitor the music played at the largest touring shows and large venues. Obviously there are thousands of venues where music is played. These range from establishments that pipe in music from services like Muzak, to stadium concerts by major artists, to county fairs. The PROs are now monitoring an ever-increasing number of large, live concert venues, in an effort to obtain accurate song performance information from this significant source of royalty income. All establishments that provide music, whether live or recorded, are required to pay performance rights fees under the copyright law. In most major cities, you can see stickers on the doors or windows of the venues that are licensed by ASCAP or BMI. SESAC is less active in enforcing these rights, but both of the other performing rights groups hire people who seek to enforce the public performance licensing requirements of the copyright law. The license fees that the establishments are required to pay are based on admission fees, the capacity of the venue, and the number of nights per week that there is live or recorded music.

When a song that is represented by a PRO is performed, the venue owner is in technical violation of the Copyright Act if he does not have a current Public Performance License. Non-profit organizations must also comply with the Copyright Act, and are similarly required to pay for the rights to the music that they choose to perform in their venues and at their events. As the U.S. copyright law makes clear, a venue that uses music as a means of enhancing its business environment, needs to see the payment of performing rights fees as compensation for the use of a songwriter's intellectual property, and as a legitimate part of the cost of doing business.

MYTH-BUSTER: "Performers have to pay fees to publicly perform music by other songwriters"

The copyright law is clear that the owner of an establishment where music is performed is responsible for obtaining the necessary public performance rights license. Some people mistakenly believe that musicians and entertainers must obtain licenses to perform copyrighted music at clubs, or that businesses where music is performed can shift their responsibility to obtain a Public Performance License to the musicians or entertainers. Some songwriters are also under the mistaken impression that if they perform a song by an established songwriter at a coffeehouse, that they need the writer's permission and must pay a fee. This is not true. It is the venue owner, not the performer, who is responsible for obtaining a license and paying performing rights license fees. A venue owner may elect to hire a third-party producer to produce a concert event, and the payment/reimbursement of performance rights fees may be an element of their production agreement, but, ultimately, it is the venue owner who has the responsibility to pay the Public Performance License fees.

Songwriters and the Performing Rights Organizations

A Performing Rights Organization's primary functions are to license music users, monitor song performances, and collect and distribute royalties to writers, composers, and publishers. PROs negotiate license agreements with the users of music (radio and TV stations, cable stations, concert halls, websites, etc.), which give the user the right to perform the music and lyrics of any member of these organizations. The license fees collected are distributed to the writers and music publishers whose works are performed and picked up in surveys in the licensed areas. The financial importance of the performing rights area cannot be overemphasized for writers and publishers. ASCAP currently has two programs that are of special value to songwriters. A unique financial program for the benefit of writer-artists is ASCAPLUS. The ASCAPLUS Awards Program is for writer members of any genre whose performances are primarily in venues not surveyed; and/or writer members whose catalogues have prestige value for which they would not otherwise be compensated. ASCAPLUS Awards are based on panel review of recent activity of writer applicants. Each applicant is considered on merit and in the context of all others applying. ASCAPLUS is not a contest or competition involving the critical evaluation of any specific work or works. The primary basis for panel determinations is the activity generated by each member's catalogue, with emphasis on recent performances. The only requirements to participate in this program are that the writer cannot have received more than $15,000.00 in ASCAP distributions in that year, and an application must be submitted which lists the writer's song performance activities and performances during the last year. As we have pointed out, many songwriters write in niche areas of music that the PROs may not survey, making these supplemental distributions a good-faith payment of approximate airplay royalties. BMI does not have a similar supplemental royalty distribution program at this time, but does sponsor other worthwhile songwriter programs and events. SESAC has a program that compensates writers with a small advance for any song that is on a recording that is in national release or distribution. ASCAP also sponsors a national music critic's award that is given for the year's best books and magazine articles. The award includes both a check and a plaque, and is obviously a great credit for someone writing about music.

In addition to the collection and distribution of royalties, PROs can also be helpful to writers in a number of creative, promotional, and educational ways. The "Membership Department" in each of the organizations produces educational workshops, seminars, and showcases. Both ASCAP and BMI conduct such workshops regularly in New York, Nashville, and Los Angeles, and they also routinely sponsor educational seminars in conjunction with the major music conferences and festivals held throughout the United States and Canada. ASCAP Showcases include ASCAP/MAC Cabaret Songwriters Showcase; ASCAP Presents (in Los Angeles, New York, Chicago, Atlanta, Miami, Nashville, and other cities); The ASCAP Foundation Presents . . . Thru The Walls; and ASCAP Presents . . . Quiet On The Set (in Los Angeles and New York).

BMI produces showcases at major industry gatherings, spotlighting developing acts, for invited audiences of record company executives, music publishers, and artist managers. BMI also sponsors a series of professional workshops in a variety of genres, including the BMI Jazz Composers Workshop; the BMI Lehman Engel Musical Theater Workshop; the BMI Songwriters Workshop; and the BMI Conductors Workshop.

ASCAP and BMI also each produce annual film-scoring workshops, introducing a select number of composers to an intensive series of educational and hands-on classes about the fundamentals of film scoring, orchestration, and conducting. And each of the PROs publishes magazines which highlight the achievements of their writer and publisher members. Today, all three of the Performing Rights Organizations remain very active in assisting and promoting their writer members.

Choosing a Performing Rights Organization

The choice as to which PRO to join is an entirely personal, subjective decision for each composer and songwriter. Every U.S. writer is free to select either ASCAP or BMI as their Performing Rights Organization. Unlike the two other Performing Rights Organizations, SESAC has a selection process by which it accepts songwriters and publishers. Songwriter submissions are reviewed by SESAC's Writer/Publisher Relations staff, and only selected writers are accepted for membership to SESAC. The details of the application process and relevant materials are available at each of the PROs' websites. Writers are strongly encouraged to contact all three societies when making the decision concerning which PRO to join. Although there are practical, philosophical, and financial considerations at play, often-times the decision to join one PRO over another rests on a personal relationship between a writer and the creative team at the organization. There are two primary questions involved in this choice: (1) which PRO is going to collect and distribute more royalties?; and (2) which is going to assist more actively in promoting a songwriter's career?

Accessing Performing Rights Organizations

In the section above, we discussed the value of establishing relationships with the people who work at PROs. We thought we would provide two different perspectives on how this can be accomplished. Dick's perspective is that of a songwriter, while Ron is an entertainment attorney, and held various positions, including Director of Business Affairs and V.P., at ASCAP, for 16 years.

Songwriter's view

I started out as a BMI writer for no particular reason. I knew that BMI was formed by the broadcasting companies in an attempt to reduce licensing fees, and that they welcomed writers in the country, folk, and jazz areas that were not welcome in ASCAP when BMI was formed in 1939. I became a recording artist and studio musician, and received some payments from BMI, generally from foreign airplay.

When I left New York and moved to Colorado, I attended a music business conference in the late 1970s that was sponsored by BMI. I asked the panel a question which intrigued Marv Mattis, the BMI executive who had provided the speakers for the panel. This led to a long-term friendship, and Marv helped provide resources for seminars and conferences in the Denver area, and opened some doors for me that got material that I wrote and/or produced listened to by people who would not have answered my phone calls.

About ten years later, I was a panelist at a songwriting seminar in Los Angeles, and Ron Sobel, an ASCAP executive, introduced himself to me. Since then, as Marv retired, I moved over to ASCAP, and Ron helped me to understand the ASCAPlus system, and he also opened some doors at record companies that were not accepting unsolicited material. That is one of the things that a PRO executive can do—his or her interest moves your material out of the "unsolicited," category.

Both of the people mentioned in the above paragraphs traveled extensively. Their role in the organizations was to assist regional music scenes outside the music business centers, and of course they also wanted to sign talented writers to their particular PRO. If you attend SXSW, MIDEM, or the various music business conferences in such places as Portland, Philadelphia, Atlanta, and Toronto, you will encounter representatives from ASCAP, BMI, and SESAC. They are generally staffing some sort of booth or exhibition table. This is your opportunity to meet them, and to initiate a relationship. When business takes you to a city where representatives are located, you should take the opportunity to follow up on your initial meeting. You can make appointments by email or phone. You should understand that these people are quite busy, so that you have to figure out the fine line between getting them to return calls, and being so aggressive that they will continue to ignore your requests.

You should not become discouraged, because it is the job of these people to bring writers into their organization, and they necessarily must always seek out fresh talent. Each of these groups has people who are active in different musical genres, from hip-hop to classical music. They also have people who specialize in music for film and television. It behooves you to cultivate relationships with whichever PRO you choose to join.

Former ASCAP exec's view

With nearly 600 employees, ASCAP has departments devoted to royalties, accounting, legal affairs, governmental affairs, foreign relations, classical music, technology, broadcaster and venue licensing, and "New Members." During my sixteen years at ASCAP, in various capacities, the primary concern for those of us in the "Membership Department" was to meet with songwriters and composers, educate them about music royalties and the bene-fits of ASCAP membership, and assist (when possible) in the advancement of their writing endeavors. My counterparts at BMI and SESAC had similar objectives, and we enjoyed a healthy and honest competition to recruit writers.

Every U.S. writer must make a Performing Rights Organization decision: ASCAP, BMI, or SESAC. The motivations and factors guiding a writer's decision can be as varied as the songs that he writes, and can result in profound impacts on a writer's career. When timing, chemistry, and talent coalesce between writer and

PRO exec, however, careers can catapult, and life-long friendships evolve. Whether booked on prominent industry Showcases, shopped to record companies, or introduced to gifted collaborators, talented writers and artists have benefited greatly from the efforts of PRO Membership executives. For other writers, it may not be exposure or connections which are needed most, but, rather, assistance in unraveling royalty distributions or song ownership registrations. Given the complexities and vagaries of Title Registrations, cue sheet registrations, and songwriter splits, it is not uncommon for hundreds of thousands of dollars in royalties to be at risk of technical or human error. The responsive and artful PRO exec can be instrumental in safeguarding, coordinating, and recovering substantial royalty sums on behalf of a writer-member. Although each of the societies has unique strengths and weaknesses—royalty plusses and minuses, organizational plusses and minuses—the personal relationships that are developed by writers with their PRO can play an enormous role in the success of a career.

In echoing the sentiments of my co-author, above, I strongly encourage composers of all stripes to actively investigate all of their potential PRO options. Phone calls, visits, web research, and recommendations from other writers and publishers will go a long way in helping to determine which PRO may be more appropriate for an individual's career. The Performing Rights Organizations can be an incredible first step in launching an emerging songwriter's professional activities, and they can be equally valuable in supporting and advancing an established writer's career. Take the time to make the phone call.

4 Publishing companies

Anyone can become a music publisher. Every songwriter and composer is a de facto publisher, by virtue of creating a musical work: a writer or composer owns the "writer share" and the "publisher share" at the point of creation. It is not until a writer voluntarily chooses to enter into a publishing deal with a third-party publisher that there is a division between writer and publisher. The breadth and depth of expertise among publishers, however, is nearly as varied as the genres of music that they represent. A music publisher deals in the marketing, commercial exploitation, and administration of songs. Originally, the term referred to publishers of sheet music, but this has changed largely over the years, and today's music publishers rarely deal with printed sheet music (those who do have come to be known as "music print publishers"). Music publishers regularly handle and control the rights to uses of musical works, and act on behalf of songwriters in matters of distributing royalties and protection against copyright infringement. As the music industry has evolved from sheet music and piano rolls to vinyl records to compact discs to MP3s and beyond, music publishers have remained committed to working to achieve the best possible compensation for their copyright owners.

There are three principal business formations for a publishing company: Sole Proprietorships, operated by a single owner, Partnerships between two or more owners, and Corporations and LLCs (Limited Liability Corporations). Each of these ownership structures has its advantages and disadvantages. Sole Proprietorships are one-person companies, where a single individual has control of all business aspects of a company, together with all profits or liabilities. Partnerships share these tasks with two or more people. Corporations offer the advantage of protecting the owners from liability, but also involve a good deal of time-consuming paperwork. Limited Liability Corporations are a compromise, creating some of the same protections that a Corporation enjoys, without all of the onerous legal requirements. For more details about these different ways of doing business, see Frank Jermance and Dick Weissman's book, *Navigating the Music Business*.

Functions of music publishing companies

Music publishers are primarily responsible for actively promoting a songwriter's talents, pitching songs to recording artists, securing synchronization placements for film or TV usages, supervising the collection and distribution of domestic and global publishing royalties, and handling copyright registration matters. Some music publishers also provide enhanced, broader services: taking a lead role in the recording and production of demos for writer-artists, and actively promoting indie and regional exposure of their writers. Regardless of its size, any reputable music publisher will ensure that its writers are adequately and fairly compensated for the use of their music. A publisher, in essence, takes care of a songwriter's music business, allowing the music creator to focus on what she does best: create.

Publishers also offer their key writers financial advances—cash payments paid in anticipation of earning future royalty income. The amount and nature of the financial payments to writers are negotiable, based on the potential writing success that the publisher envisions for its writer. Other financial incentives can include a demo recording fund, expense money to attend music conferences or co-writing sessions, and a promotional/marketing fund to assist in gaining exposure for a particular song, album, or writer-artist's performance career.

A full-service music publishing company is comprised of an Executive/Business Affairs team, a Creative Department, and an Administration Department. The Business Affairs team prepares publishing contracts, coordinates foreign and print collection deals, and may be involved in acquiring existing catalogues from other writers and music publishing companies. The Creative Department (1) actively reviews song submissions from potential new writers; (2) is primarily responsible for exploiting the songs in their catalogue; and (3) will assist their writer-artists to obtain a record deal. The "songpluggers" of the Creative Department (previously known as the "professional department") also meet and work with songwriters, discussing possible changes to songs, and setting up collaborations with other songwriters. The Administration Department coordinates all aspects of song registration (with PROs) and copyright filing (with the U.S. Copyright Office), and also oversees licensing matters, royalty collections from song users and licensees, and the timely distribution of royalties to writers.

Getting songs recorded

REALWORLD: **The Other Great Wall**

The Great Wall in China was built to protect the borders of the Chinese Empire from foreign invaders. The mythical divide between the music industry and the creative community can surely be seen as The Other Great Wall. Whether a writer is trying to have her songs listened to by a publisher, or an artist is trying to have his self-produced CD listened to by a label, there are barriers, protocols, and institutions which can make the process seemingly inscrutable. Indeed, there are several practical reasons why the industry is not entirely open and accessible to hearing new music: exposure to possible infringement allegations, coupled with the sheer amount of music that flows in, mandates a de facto "filtering" system. And from a purely practical consideration, there simply are not enough hours in a day to effectively listen to all the new music that is submitted, or which is accessible through MySpace, CD Baby, iTunes, and several other viable music sites. The challenges of getting new music to the ears of the professionals can, indeed, be daunting. More important to remember, however, is what lies on the other side of the "wall": an industry that unequivocally relies on new music. Labels and publishers won't abandon the artists that they are currently working on, but the industry always has its eye on cultivating the "next project." Great songwriters, great songs, and great artists fuel the music industry. Label executives, publishing executives,

> lawyers, agents, radio, film and television production enti-
> ties all have insatiable appetites for music. Notwithstanding
> the existence of The Other Great Wall, the real key is find-
> ing ingenious ways of taking unique art through the cracks
> and over the top, to an eager and willing industry on the
> other side.

The primary creative job of today's music publisher is song
"exploitation": (1) pitching new material by their writers to suitable recording artists to record them, with the intent of creating a
hit record and generating large numbers of sales and airplay; and
(2) pitching writers' songs for use in other media, such as television, film, commercials, and movie soundtracks.

"Exploitation":

1. The positive act of employing an asset to the greatest possible
   advantage: exploitation of songs for use in films.
2. The act of making some creative work or composition more
   valuable, profitable, productive, or useful.

There are a number of ways for a publisher to facilitate this
process.

- The publisher must develop a network of A&R (artist and
  repertoire) record company contacts.
- The publisher needs to maintain data bases of artists and
  independent producers.
- The publisher subscribes to Tip Sheets, such as *New on the
  Charts*.
- The publisher needs to maintain a network of personal
  managers and music business attorneys.

A publisher that has personal contact with a recording artist is
much more apt to get songs a good hearing than someone who is
always approaching the artist through one of the artist's representatives, like a lawyer or a manager. Sometimes record producers like to write songs with outside writers, and such a demo
is much more apt to get the artist's attention. Sometimes this
requires the publisher to split the publishing with the producer, in
other instances the producer may end up signed to the music

publisher's record company. Obviously connections with successful record producers are valuable in today's music industry.

Tip Sheets are industry publications that list the projects that artists and producers are working on, and what types of songs they are looking for. An example of a Tip Sheet listing might be "Alice Smith is recording a country-folk project and is looking for folk ballads with a beat. Demos should be sent to Arthur Jones at PDQ Productions, 125 Maple St., Nashville TN., 56666. No phone calls or emails, please." They can be useful and save time, in the sense that if a country artist is doing a Latin album, for example, there isn't much point in pitching that artist a bluegrass tune. There are dozens of other publishers and songwriters reading the same Tip Sheets, so the information is not as exclusive as you might hope it would be.

Personal managers and music business attorneys are in constant contact with recording artists, and so they need to be cultivated as sources and contacts, as well. As new genres of music develop and move in and out of popularity, a well-rounded publisher will be able to provide songs to artists in each of those genres. Music industry functions, such as seminars, award dinners, or even parties, are opportunities for the music publisher to network with all of the various music business professionals listed above.

Other publisher functions and interactions

Large publishing companies that own and control thousands of copyrights also spend a considerable amount of time and energy re-evaluating the existing songs that are in their catalogues. It's very likely that a publisher will make modern or updated demo recordings of older works in their catalogue. An evergreen, like a Cole Porter song, has been recorded numerous times. It's a challenge, however, to update an older song in such a way that it fits into the contemporary music market. An innovative publisher will commission new demos that showcase such songs in a more contemporary musical style. Publishers will also print folios, book-style collections of songs, and CD compilations of their songs, which are not intended to be sold, but are sent to industry executives who may be interested to record the song, or place it in a film, television show, or commercial.

REALWORLD: Sister Gertrude Morgan

One very innovative publisher took an interest in Sister Gertrude Morgan (1900–1980), a painter, singer, and self-proclaimed "bride of Christ," whose visually explosive folk art is celebrated on the world-wide museum circuit. But her one album, made in New Orleans in the 1960s, is one of black gospel music's secret relics. Those recordings were unearthed, and a limited number of copies were released to unanimous and widespread critical acclaim in 2003. In a joint venture with Ropeadope Records, the publisher and label procured the master rights and enlisted internationally acclaimed DJ and producer King Britt to create an entirely new and ground-breaking work, putting musical tracks behind the Sister's previously unaccompanied vocals. In the studio for over twelve months working on this project, King hired a crew of stellar musicians to create the ultimate backing band and produced a ground-breaking CD featuring gospel hymns, funk, soul melodies, and deep percussive beats. Through the efforts of one publisher, songs, many of which are more than forty years old, or in the public domain, have been reintroduced into the commercial marketplace, and are creating revenue streams for artists, publishers, writers, musicians, and record companies.

Music publishers also will sometimes assist their writer-artists in the promotion of a CD release. Of course, this only occurs when the publisher controls the publishing on all or most of the songs. If a music publisher has a song that is a hit in a specific genre, for example gospel music, and the song shows signs of breaking through in the pop market, the publisher may be quite willing to spend money to help promote the song to a cross-over market. The performance rights on a broad-based pop hit generates much more income than a song that is only on the gospel chart, so the publisher is investing in promotion and exposure that might result in higher performance income, and ultimately more CD sales and mechanical royalties. Publishing deals, therefore, can be tailor-made to an individual writer's goals. The combination of a relatively small financial investment, coupled with a visionary plan for exposure or promotion, can have very significant results on a writer's career.

Holds

When a song is submitted to an artist or a producer, if that person likes the song, he will ask the publisher or writer to place a "hold" on it. This is a verbal commitment that indicates that the person holding the song either wants to listen to it more closely, or has already decided that he wishes to record it. People in the business differ on the level of commitment that a hold represents. Some take the position that if a song is on hold they will not shop it to other artists or producers. Several problems may occur under this scenario. One is that the person holding the song may forget about it, or simply be indecisive as to whether he really wishes to record it. Certainly if a song is on hold for months and months, it is appropriate to start showing it to others. Beyond the problem of holds is the situation surrounding the actual recording. Some artists are notorious for over-recording. What we mean by this term is that the artist has decided to do, for example, twelve songs on an album, but they have recorded seventeen songs. The artist has indeed recorded your song, but unfortunately for you, your song wasn't included in the final release. Co-author Dick Weissman once wrote an R&B song that a major producer-arranger loved. The producer placed the song on hold, and indeed recorded it with a new artist that he was quite excited about. Unfortunately, the singer froze in the studio, and the producer never got any satisfactory performances out of her. The artist was dropped from her contract with a major label, and the producer-arranger then forgot about the song and the artist.

REALWORLD: "It ain't final 'till it's vinyl" (circa 1988)

A very prominent artist in the 1980s was seeking songs for the follow-up record to her previous multi-platinum release. Publishers, of course, were very eager to submit songs for consideration for this record. Mechanical royalties for a song included on another multi-platinum selling record would surely generate more than $200,000.00, and performance royalties from a possible radio hit single could generate another $300,000.00. Clearly, having a song picked for this record would be a financial windfall, and a writer's dream. It was a very good day when the label called the publisher, requesting a hold on a specific song for this highly anticipated new record. This, of course, is a great start, but it does not guarantee that the song will be recorded or included in the final release. After all, prior to the advent of CDs, it was a well-known mantra in the publishing community that "it ain't final 'till it's vinyl." After months of continued song searches and recording, the label called with the confirmation that the song was recorded, and would, indeed, be included in the final release! With an initial sales target of two million units, it was clearly time to pop the champagne. Several weeks later, the record, with the publisher's song, was released to great reviews. Within days of the release, however, the publisher received a call from the label: the artist and producer had come across a new song—after the record had been released—that they were convinced was "an absolute smash single which needed to be included on the album." The label was so convinced about the strength of the new song, that they made the extraordinary decision to recall the already-released record, and re-manufacture the album, so as to include the additional track. That's the good news. But the label also decided that one of the existing tracks would need to be bumped off the record to accommodate the new song. Yup. The publisher's song was stripped from the final-final release. (The new song did go on to become a Top Five radio staple, contributing to multi-multi-platinum album sales). Although "holds" are a very good thing, today, it may not be final until it's . . .

Collaborations

Collaborating with other writers is primarily a creative endeavor of art, craft, and skill. Where composers can create scores by themselves, many songwriters choose to concentrate on their lyric writing, while others choose to concentrate on writing music and melodies. In other situations, both (or all) of the co-writers contribute, in varying degrees, to the overall process and evolution of the final song. There are numerous books written on the craft of songwriting, which we encourage aspiring writers to read. These books often suggest that collaborators should "write up." In other words, writers should seek to find more advanced or skilled writers as collaborators. In much the same way that a tennis player will not improve her game if she always plays with a weaker partner, writers can be challenged, and develop, by writing with a more experienced partner.

As artful as the songwriting process is, however, it also should be seen as a joint business venture—a partnership, of sorts— where very significant amounts of money and acclaim can flow to the "co-creators/co-owners." There is a common understanding among songwriters that the writing "ownership"—the percentage of ownership in the completed song—will be split evenly among those "in the room" during the writing session. This is easily accomplished where there is one lyricist, and one melody/music writer: 50 percent ownership is attributed to each collaborator. Even where a song is "equally written" by three writers, allocating the ownership in a three-way split is easily accomplished. But some collaborations cannot easily be categorized as "words by Jane" and "music by Tom." Indeed, one contributor may come in with a great title that drives a writing session, but does not contribute any additional lyrics. One writer may come in with a great chorus (lyric or music), but doesn't contribute anything additional to the song. There are limitless possibilities in the creation of a song among collaborators. And there are fair agreements among the writers that can be employed to clarify the ownership of each song. Each writing session—and each group of writers—should have an understanding of how the song credits will be split. In order to avoid confusion, argument, or lawsuit at a later date, it is strongly encouraged that the writers agree to the ownership shares, in writing, at the conclusion of the session. A simple, signed "song-split" memo will serve to clarify all of the ownership, registration, and royalty issues "for the life of the composer(s), plus seventy years." And, in the absence of a third-party publishing agreement, the "publisher share" of a song is usually equal to the "writer share" for each writer, making the fair allocation of ownership, and royalties, just that much more important. It's just as likely that writers will choose to make an equal allocation of ownership among all of the writers in the room, as they will to make an effort to attribute writer shares according to actual contribution. One platinum-selling band, where songs were written by a "committee of five," literally counted the words—not lines—that each member contributed to a completed song: 17 words out of 77, resulted in a 22 percent share of the lyric portion; 51 words earned a 66 percent share of the lyric, and 9 words earned a 12 percent share. (If hundreds of thousands of dollars in royalties are at stake, small percentages will make a difference.) Picking collaborators may be more difficult than meets the eye.

Collaborations with producers and artists

Successful record producers have direct access to writer-artists in the studio, and non-writer recording artists are always looking for great songs to record. Often-times, spontaneous "collaborations" or song interpretations can occur between the producer and the artist in the studio.

Difficult situations can arise when a producer or artist claims that her contribution in the studio is sufficient to earn a co-writing or co-publishing position in the song. There is a fine line, however, between writing a song, and adding instrumental parts which may merely alter the sound of a work.

It's important that writers, artists, and producers communicate clearly and fairly about the nature and scope of each person's involvement and contribution to a finished song. Writers have been put in very awkward situations when major recording artists claim to have "re-worked" a song in the studio, and therefore seek to obtain a co-writer's ownership position in a song . . . "in order for the track to be included on the record." It presents a very difficult moral, ethical, and financial dilemma for a writer to consider granting a co-writer/co-publishing interest in a song to a major artist who had very little involvement in writing the actual song. The financial prospects of owning "half" of a song which is included on a platinum-selling record, in addition to the publicity of sharing a "co-writing credit" with a major artist goes a long way to challenging a writer's integrity. Does this ever happen? You will find Elvis Presley's name as the co-author of a number of songs, although there is very little evidence that he ever wrote any songs. Dick Weissman has a friend who once sang a song for a young artist who said he "loved" the song. The artist added that he would record the song . . . if he could write a bridge for it.

The writer felt that the artist's demand, which was presented as an aesthetic choice, was actually an attempt by the artist to include himself as a songwriter and copyright owner. The writer turned down the opportunity. The album that the song would have appeared on ended up being a multi-platinum seller. From a strictly financial viewpoint, clearly Weissman's friend made a major error. On the other hand, the writer retained the entire ownership of the song. Unfortunately, the song never was recorded by another artist.

Song critiques and dealing with rejection

When a writer's songs are critiqued at organizational meetings, no matter who is providing the feedback, the best option is to listen, and learn, without having an immediate emotional reaction. It is always possible to conclude later that the person doing the critique is absolutely wrong. At the Liverpool Institute of Performing Arts, in England (LIPA), a member of a songwriting class had taken some very tough and specific criticism of one of his songs from the teacher. By coincidence one day, Paul McCartney, who went to elementary school in the building that LIPA is housed in, offered to do some one-on-one critiques with students. It turned out that the things the teacher had thought needed improvement in the student's song, were exactly the things that Paul liked about it. One person's opinion is just that.

A writer should also not be offended if the person providing the song critiques only listens to a portion of the song. Whether there are time restrictions at the event, or the critic simply hears something that signals a strength or weakness in the song, it is an unfortunate fact that many songs are not listened to in their entirety. This is a fact both at live events, and within the offices of music executives.

Some writers have the skill and gift to create amazing lyrics and/or melodies, but they may be a bit deficient in the area of "self-editing." It often takes an objective, professional ear to evaluate songs from a commercial or market perspective. There is a considerable amount of psychology involved here. Much like the role that a coach or trainer has with his students, the rapport that is created between a writer and his critic, publisher, or co-writer, can contribute to a positive experience and a learning opportunity.

At the same time that a writer should be receptive to criticism, she should not necessarily make significant changes to her song simply because of one person's criticism of a melody or lyric. Give the critique some thought, play the song for several other people, and then decide whether a change will improve the song. No one likes everything, and what one person may think of as a profound lyric, may strike another listener (or critic) as being ordinary and banal. When discouraged, console yourself with the fact that the Beatles were turned down by every record company in England, twice, before their manager made contact with George Martin.

Who do publishers sign?

Notwithstanding the concentration of gifted writers living in the major music cities of Los Angeles, New York, Nashville, Atlanta, and Miami, it's clear that publishers may be interested to sign a writer who lives in Boise, if the material is compelling, the creative work ethic is strong, and there is a commitment to help the publisher to execute innovative and strategic marketing plans for the songs. It's also important that the creative goals and expectations of the writer match the professional expertise of the publisher. The publisher who has a great reputation and a successful track record getting country songs covered, may not be effective in getting rock songs covered. It's not likely, therefore, that the country music publisher would be interested in signing a great rock songwriter. Indeed, most rock and alternative artists write their own material, which has limited the opportunities for "outside writers" and their publishers to submit songs to rock artists. The same is becoming true in other genres, as well. While Nashville remains the last stronghold where recording artists and their producers routinely seek out great songs and great song-writers, the growing market for film, television, and advertising music is keeping talented writers and their publishers challenged and employed.

Above all else, publishers are looking for truly gifted, committed creators. Casual hobbyists need not apply. Whether a writer is a self-contained singer-songwriter-producer, or is simply a master lyricist seeking collaborations with a melody writer, professional music publishers have set high standards when considering who to sign.

REALWORLD: "On a scale from 1 to 10 . . ."

Songwriting is not science. Skill, craft, and experience are certainly key ingredients in the process, but art, inspiration, and spirit are also equal partners. There are numerous books available on the craft of songwriting, and yet, the mechanics of "success" are much more elusive. Clearly, melody and lyric are the heartbeat of a song. But lyrical message, point of view, passion, uniqueness, creativity, and prosody (*"the relationship between the lyrics, melody, and rhythms of a song"*) are the subtle underpinnings of great songs. Hearing a special song from a young writer—in demo form, live off the stage, or as a produced Master Recording—is a rare and wondrous experience. Hearing a collection of several special songs from an individual creator is that much more infrequent. In various industry capacities over the years, we've had the good fortune to hear the music of literally thousands of aspiring songwriters, composers, and artists. With apologies in advance to our songwriter friends, if the music we've listened to from emerging writers over the years were evaluated "on a scale from 1 to 10," unfortunately, most of the songs have been a 3: unstructured, uninspired, uncreative, un-special, and, ultimately, un-important. It's a good day when we come across a 5 or 6. At the moment that we hear an 8, the hairs stand up on the back of our neck. An 8 is truly rare, and is indicative of greater potential. But when considering whether to sign a new writer to a publishing contract, and whether to invest a substantial amount of money, time, and staff resources into promoting a young writer's career in a highly competitive marketplace, a publisher will ask herself, "while surrounded with truly gifted songwriters, does the world really need another 7"?

The nature and role of demos

The publisher generally advances the money to make professional-sounding demos of songs that a writer submits. In the music business centers, there is a core of musicians who are readily available to make demos, who sing and/or play new material quickly and accurately. If the songwriter is new to the town, the publisher can provide the writer with the names of people who have these skills. In some cases the publishing company owns their own recording studio, which will facilitate the process of making demos from the standpoint of the songwriter being familiar with the recording engineer. It is not unusual at a large publishing company for writers to trade services on each other's demos. A writer who is a skilled singer might sing on another writer's demo, and in return the second writer might play bass on the other writer's demos.

As home studios have proliferated, many writers possess the capability of making excellent demos without the need for paying studio rental fees. If the songwriter is also the music publisher, this becomes even more useful, as we will see in Chapter 6.

Every songwriter, to advance her career, will need to make a demo recording of her material. There are myriad reasons to make a demo, all of them compelling. A key rule in recording a demo: the songwriter needs to make a good demo of the *song*, while the artist needs to make a good recording of the *performance* of the song.

A "songwriter's demo" can be as simple as a piano/vocal recording. A great lyric, coupled with a compelling melody, doesn't need big production values to be understood and appreciated. Indeed, most publishers, when evaluating new writers and their songs, prefer to hear a basic recording of the material. Multi-tracked instruments and layered vocals are simply unnecessary to convey the passion and uniqueness of a special song. The words, chords, and melody should be able to speak for themselves. Often-times, an over-produced "song demo" may telegraph that the writer is either not confident in the strength of the stand-alone song, or that the "writer" is really showcasing his producer skills, as opposed to his songwriter skills. If the intent is to showcase and present one's craft and skill as a songwriter, a stripped-down recording will always be sufficient. It is also true, however, that publishers now tend to sign "hyphens": writer-producers, singer-songwriters, or writer-artists. In this case, the demo submitted to these publishers must showcase not only great writing, but the other hyphenated talents, as well.

If, on the other hand, the demo's function is to showcase an aspiring "artist" or "producer," that recording must capture the attitude, texture, sound, and charisma of the talent. Record companies need to hear what a prospective band, artist, or producer sounds like when recorded, and they expect to receive "demos" that accurately paint a picture that reflects the full scope of talent being offered. A rock band needs to sound like a rock band on their demo, while a hip-hop producer needs to sound like . . . a hip-hop producer.

Cross-collateralization of income

"Cross-collateralization" clauses can be included in publishing and recording agreements, affecting both writers and artists. In the case of a songwriter, the cross-collateralization clause is a statement included in a publishing contract that would permit the publisher to take royalties and revenues otherwise due and payable to the writer from one song, and apply them towards any unpaid recoupable advances or outstanding costs incurred from another song. The typical clause in an agreement contains this language: "company may recoup advances from royalties to be paid to you or on your behalf pursuant to this Agreement or any other agreement between you and company's affiliates." This clause gives the company the right to recoup advances from royalties that writers or artists receive not only under the current contract, but all other agreements with the company, past and future. One consequence may be that a songwriter who has had one successful song may not receive any royalties because they would be used to offset losses incurred from other endeavors— demo recording expenses, travel expenses, and promotion or marketing expenses. The very same clause can have the same effect for recording artists: there is no link of particular advances and particular royalties to particular albums. All advances are recoupable from all royalties generated from all prior projects with that company. Depending on the wording of this and other clauses, a cross-collateralization clause can have direct, deceiving, and often very undesirable consequences to a writer when applied in conjunction with other clauses of the contract.

Publishing administration

The "administration" services that a publisher provides for its writers generally include the technical copyright, registration, filing, licensing, and global royalty collection activities that are required to safeguard the ownership and maximize the income of a song. The "admin" functions of a publisher generally do not include any of the creative or pitching aspects that are provided by the other departments. The Administration Agreement establishes a relationship whereby the writer retains her copyright ownership in the songs, but engages the publisher/administrator to perform the business and collection aspects of the songs in her catalogue, in exchange for a fee. After deducting this administration fee (10 to 20 percent of the gross proceeds), the administrator distributes 100 percent of the remaining net income to the songwriter. The "admin" songwriter typically has existing activity and success for her songs, and does not want or need a publisher to proactively promote her catalogue. An administrator does not participate in the ownership of the copyright, per se. All rights and ownership, including creative exploitation, remain with the songwriter. There are advantages for a writer to retain the copyright to her songs, as an administration deal can provide an artist with greater financial and artistic control. And, where writers seek the assistance of an administrator to promote their songs, an increased "placement" fee will be charged on income earned from obtaining covers or placements. An administration deal generally has an initial term of three years, with an option to renew thereafter.

Songsharks: *caveat emptor*

Songshark is the common slang term for the most unscrupulous type of music "publisher." Songsharks make their profit not on royalties from sales, but by charging inexperienced writers for "services" (some real, such as demo recording or musical arranging, some fictional, such as "audition" or "review" fees) that a legitimate publisher provides without cost to the writer. Songsharks aren't concerned with royalties or long-term profit, and do little if any actual promotion of songs; rather, they devote themselves to bilking as many writers as they can, in exchange for making demo recordings of writers' lyrics set to stock, production tracks.

Songsharks are people who try to get prospective songwriters or recording artists to record and/or publish their songs, by inducing the naïve writer or artist to pay the company a fee for these services: this is the reverse of the way the process is supposed to work. The music publisher or record company should be paying you, not the other way around.

Song information registered with the Copyright Office is available to the public. Songwriters with registered works will receive inquiries from some of these companies, stating that for x dollars they will record professional demos of the registered songs, and send them to record companies and record producers. The songsharks will usually operate legally, in the sense that they will, indeed, record the songs. The recording result will be uninspired, at best. The company will then fulfill the rest of their legal obligations by indeed mailing the songs on a CD, along with the songs of a group of other writers who were contacted in a similar way.

Sometimes these companies advertise in magazines seeking lyrics to set to music.

The most unscrupulous songsharks will take the process to an even higher level. After they make the initial demo, they will then go back to the songwriter, and explain that for an additional y dollars, they can add strings or horns or background vocals to the recording, and thus give the song a "more professional sound, which will surely result in the song becoming a monster hit." Before entering into any deal that requires the payment of money in order to have songs published, do a little investigative work about the company, and have an attorney review the papers before you sign. Buyer beware.

5 Publishing deals

Publishing contracts

People often speak of "publishing deals" in a generic way, which implies that there may only be one kind of publishing deal. In fact, there are a number of different kinds of publishing arrangements that a writer may enter into. In the days of Tin Pan Alley music publishing, songwriters simply sold the publishing rights to music publishers for a flat fee. Later, as songwriters became more business savvy and gained more negotiating leverage, a new kind of contract evolved, consisting of three basic elements: (1) an assignment of all or a portion of the copyright ownership (so-called "publisher share") of the song to the publisher; (2) an obligation on the publisher to commercially exploit the songs (e.g., by the sale of sheet music); and (3) an obligation to account for and pay royalties to the songwriter. Today, payment of standard songwriter royalties is always a part of a songwriter's Agreement, regardless of whether the contract is a "work-for-hire," a standard songwriter Agreement, or a Co-Publishing Agreement. The incentives, obligations, and ownership scenarios, however, are now entirely negotiable. The key clauses in contemporary publishing Agreements include a mutual understanding of (1) the percentage of copyright ownership and royalty participation transferred, if any; (2) the functions that the publisher will perform; and (3) the Term of the Agreement. Standard songwriter royalties include the writer's share of performance, synchronization and mechanical income, sheet music and folio income, digital download income, foreign income, and ancillary new media and merchandising royalties. Although the traditional publishing deal still widely exists today, various newer kinds of publishing arrangements have evolved over the years. And of course, as we will see in the next chapter, writers and composers are always capable of retaining 100 percent of their copyrights, and manage their publishing affairs through Self-Publishing arrangements. Publishing Agreements today include variations of:

1. The Traditional Publishing Agreement. Appropriate when a songwriter and a publisher seek to have a relationship for all of the material that the songwriter will be writing during the duration of the contract. This deal will cover material written during the Term of the contract, and may also include specified songs written before the contract was entered into. The contract will include a Delivery Requirement, requiring the songwriter to deliver a certain number of new original songs to the publisher during each year of the contract. Typically, the writer is assigning 100 percent ownership of the copyright (the so-called "publishing share") of the songs covered by the contract, while retaining 100 percent of the so-called "writer share" of income. The publisher receives all income and royalties from third parties, and then distributes the writer's share of that income to the writer. Established publishers usually pay a recoupable advance to the songwriter for the first year, and additional advances each successive year that the publisher exercises its option to continue the contract.

> ❗● A writer's decision to enter into a publishing contract—to assign up to 50 percent of the rights and revenues to an outside publisher—has long-term financial impacts. When a chart-topping song can generate more than $500,000.00 in royalties in its first year, conventional wisdom generally tells a young writer to "hold on to their publishing": sharing up to 50 percent of $500,000.00 with a publisher can seem like a pretty hefty price to pay. More often than not, however, it is the publisher who took the song to the public market . . . the publisher who obtained the artist's recording ("cover") of the song . . . or the publisher who was instrumental in placing the song in a lucrative film or television project. There are countless numbers of songwriters who currently own 100 percent of all of their songs—and who also have a career owning 100 percent of no

commercial activity and no royalty income. The opportunity, years earlier, to have engaged an active publisher and share royalties, often seems like a good idea in retrospect. With hundreds of thousands of dollars at stake, the decision to engage a publisher is perhaps the most important decision that a writer can make.

2. The Single Song Agreement. Based on the same concept and royalty distribution structure as the "traditional" type of deal mentioned above, but involves only one of the songwriter's songs (i.e., songs already written), as opposed to all of the writer's works written during the Term. The advances paid to the writer, if any, are on a song-by-song basis, and are usually a modest sum. In exchange, the publisher acquires the exclusive rights to administer and represent the song to obtain a recording, or to place it in a film or some other media.

3. The Co-Publishing Agreement. Involves a co-ownership of the publisher share of the copyright: 50 percent of the publishing interest is retained by the writer, and 50 percent of the publishing interest is assigned to the publisher (see Figure 5.1). As is the case with the traditional and the single song agreements, the writer retains 100 percent of the writer share of all royalties earned during the Term. In "co-pub" deals, therefore, the writer retains 75 percent of all income (the entire 100 percent writer share + 50 percent of the publisher share).

4. The Development Deal. Typically negotiated for an emerging writer/artist, whereby the publisher invests time and money into "developing" the writer for future projects and success. The Development (or "Step") Deal typically sets exploitation, income, placement, or sales goals ("steps"). When one of the target goals has been achieved, the writer is rewarded with an expansion of some of the positive aspects of the songwriter agreement.

5. The Administration Agreement. Establishes a relationship whereby the writer retains her copyright ownership in the songs, but engages the publisher/administrator to perform the business, copyright registration, licensing, and global royalty collection aspects of the songs in her catalogue, in exchange

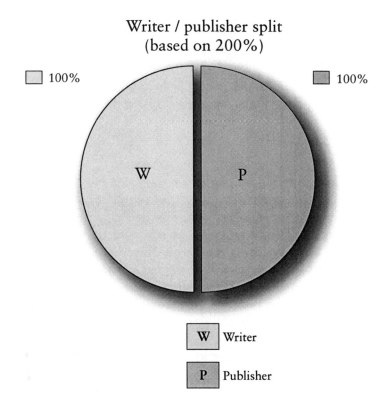

Figure 5.1 Writer / publisher split.

for a fee. After deducting this administration fee (anywhere from 10 to 20 percent of the gross proceeds), the administrator distributes 100 percent of the remaining net income to the songwriter.

6. Catalogue Representation Agreements. Useful for composers who want assistance in pitching and placing their songs in film, television, advertising, or video game opportunities. Representation deals are entirely negotiable, and can involve the payment of retainers, commissions, or copyright assignments in exchange for the placement services offered to the composer.

Publishing contract deal points

Most of the various types of music publishing contracts contain similar basic provisions covering the advance, royalty payments, copyright ownership, and warranties and representations. These are the key issues that are included in most publishing agreements:

1. Term: The duration of the agreement can be based on calendar ("contract") years or on the number of songs written and delivered. For example, the contract year Term in a staff writer deal is usually one year with a certain number of options. Another frequently encountered contract year Term would be the longer of twelve months or until a specified number of songs have been delivered. Publishing agreements are generally three to four years in duration.

2. Territory: While it may be possible for some established writers to limit the publisher's rights to certain territories by way of an "admin deal," a worldwide territory is common for single song, co-pub, and traditional publishing deals.

3. Scope and Compositions: A publishing deal can be for a single composition, a CD, or an entire catalogue. The deal can include past, present, and future songs. The "scope" clause specifies which songs are included in the deal. Writers may try to exclude previously released songs and limit the scope to songs written during the Term of the publishing agreement.

4. Advances: The "advance" is a sum of money paid by the publisher to the songwriter for conveying to the publisher copyrights to a song or a collection of agreed songs, and may be the most important issue to the writer. The amount of the advance is based on the degree to which the publisher believes that it can earn royalty income off your songs through successful exploitation. The advance is usually "non-refundable and recoupable." Once the publisher has recouped its advance and expenses, additional income collected is distributed between the writer and the publisher in accordance with the contract terms, except for the writer's public performance royalties, which are paid directly to the writer from the PRO. An advance can be structured as an automatic, "guaranteed" payment, for example, $20,000.00, due immediately upon signing the publishing agreement, or, alternatively, a "contingent advance" can be structured to be paid when specific goals are achieved, such as a single song or CD reaches certain sales, income, or chart positions. A contingent advance can also be distributed based on a percentage of earnings from previous years, using financial minimums and maximums as payment guidelines.

5. Delivery Requirement: In return for the royalty advance, a songwriter promises to deliver a certain number of "completed" musical compositions during the Term. If the contract requires the delivery of twelve songs per year, a writer who co-writes all songs, thereby retaining only a 50 percent ownership in each song, must deliver twenty-four "completed" songs to meet the requirements of the contract. Where substantial advances are involved, a music publisher often requires the submission of "commercially acceptable" songs, together with a requirement that a certain number of the writer's compositions get released on a record in the United States by a "major" record label.

6. Ownership: The ownership of the copyright is perhaps one of the most important terms in a publishing deal. Although the writer retains the 100 percent writer share, the publisher typically acquires 100 percent copyright ownership, worldwide, for life of copyright, through an assignment from the writer. The copyright owner controls the administration rights to the songs, throughout the world. No ownership rights are typically granted in admin, collection, representation, or sub-publishing agreements. The allocation of royalty income is paid according to the ownership. In a "100 percent pub deal", the writer retains 100 percent of the writer share of royalties, and the publisher retains 100 percent of the publisher share of royalties. Under a typical co-publishing deal, however, where the publisher share is co-owned—50 percent by the publisher, and 50 percent by the writer—the writer (co-publisher) retains 100 percent of the writer's share of income, and 50 percent of the publisher's share, or 75 percent of all income. Co-pub deals, therefore, are often referred to as "75–25 deals."

7. Administration: This clause grants the music publisher the right to control the business, royalty, licensing, and exploitation rights to the compositions. An "administration" fee is charged by the administrator/publisher, typically 10 to 15 percent, deducted off the top of the gross income generated by the compositions. In a Co-Administration deal, each half of the publisher share is separately administered by the owner of that portion. In the co-admin situation, the writer retains control over his portion of the royalty collection issues, as well as the creative exploitation and licensing decisions for the works. Co-publishing deals can also be structured wherein one of the two (or more) publishers is selected to be the administering publisher, thereby unifying and simplifying the process of administration.

8. Restrictions: There are a number of creative and control rights that a writer may choose not to grant to the publisher, and for which the writer may want to retain approval rights. For example, a writer may insist that her songs not be used commercially in conjunction with tobacco or alcohol companies, political advertisements, or adult film, without prior approval. A writer may not want any translations, adaptations, or arrangements of the songs granted to third parties without prior approval. Other restrictions could include limiting the publisher from commercially exploiting any demo recording, or from issuing mechanical licenses "below statutory rate." Another provision would be to preclude any synchronization licenses without approval, or no use of the title of a song on any film/TV/stage production without writer consent. A writer can sometimes also limit the publisher's right to settle copyright infringement or other lawsuits against the writer without the writer's consent. And, depending on the leverage of the writer, Grand Rights and merchandising rights can be restricted, stipulating that a publisher cannot—without the writer's permission—use songs in a theatrical dramatization, or license songs in regards to any merchandise.

9. Reversion: Under U.S. Copyright laws, the length of time a music publisher is allowed to retain ownership of and/or administrative rights to the post-1978 copyrights acquired during the duration of the publishing agreement is thirty-five years. At the end of the thirty-five-year Term, the ownership of the copyrights fully return ("revert") back to the writer. The provision that specifies the writer's right to regain the copyrights is called a "reversion clause." Depending on several factors in a publishing relationship, some music publishers agree to revert copyrights to writers after a seven- or ten-year Term. Reversions only occur, of course, when any advances paid to the writer are fully recouped.

A reversion clause may also be triggered when a publisher commits a substantial breach of the terms of the deal, or fails to pay the royalties properly or on a timely basis.

Evaluating a publisher

If a young songwriter is talented enough, and lucky enough, to receive an offer from a publishing company, it can be daunting to objectively evaluate the terms of the deal and the nature of the company. Every publisher has different strengths, weaknesses, and creative strategies.

❗ The threshold question for every songwriter is whether to enter into a publishing deal. Colloquial euphemism has reduced the answer to: "don't give away your publishing." This oversimplification misses the point by a long shot. Yes, the publishing "half" of a song is very valuable. For each dollar that the "writer half" of a song earns, the "publisher half" earns its own dollar. A chart-topping song can earn $200,000.00 for the writer share, and another $200,000.00 for the publisher share. No one would be expected to "give away" a publisher share that has value. The answer, therefore, is not a matter of "giving away" something of value, but rather, one of determining the value of the publishing portion of a song, and negotiating a fair exchange for the "potential value" of the publishing rights. The publishing rights in an unexploited song do not have much current financial value—there is no income stream flowing from the song. If the song becomes successful, however, the publishing rights do become very valuable. The key word: "if." Or, more appropriately, "how" can a song become successful . . . how can it generate income? This is precisely what a publisher does. The successful publisher promotes, exploits, manages, and administrates on behalf of the song, bringing royalties, license income, and value to the copyright.

For the songwriter who can perform the creative and administrative functions of a publisher, there may be little reason to enter into a publishing deal. For those writers, however, who choose to focus on their writing, and who choose not to enter the media-business marketplace of pitching, placing, licensing, and collecting royalties, a publisher serves as a perfect partner. One partner creates, utilizing her gifts and expertise as a writer, and the other partner promotes and manages the business activities of the song, utilizing her gifts and expertise as music and media executive.

The true equation, therefore, becomes one in which the savvy writer chooses to "hire" a publisher to perform the business activities for the songs. The currency paid by the writer to hire the publisher: an interest in the publishing share of the song! A writer doesn't "give away" her publishing rights. A serious writer, seeking to breathe life and activity into her songs—and her writing career—will hire and purchase the necessary business and publishing expertise with the potential capital represented by a portion of the publishing rights to her songs (see Figure 5.2).

Generally, a number of factors come into consideration in evaluating a publishing offer:

- What, if any, are the monetary advances?
- Are there provisions for demo recording, travel, and promotion funds?
- Does the creative team at the company share the career goals of the writer?
- What success has the company had with other writers' songs?
- Is there a reversion clause?
- Is there an opportunity to enter a co-publishing agreement?

Where a writer is seeking financial stability, an "exclusive staff writer's deal" provides the most security, in exchange for a larger share of the copyright and publishing interest. In this arrangement, if the publisher's critiques don't make any sense to you, there is every reason to expect that when money comes into play, the conflicts will increase. Not every publisher can relate to a Lyle Lovett. If you expect someone to promote and subsidize your music, it's best that they have a fundamental understanding of

Co-writer / co-publisher splits
(based on 200%)

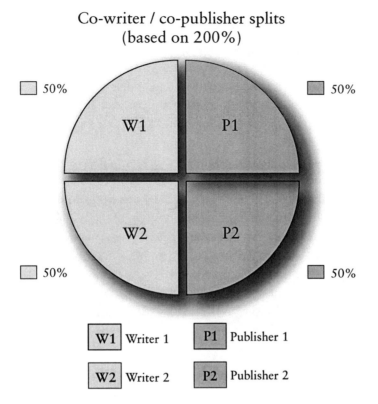

50%   W1   P1   50%

50%   W2   P2   50%

| W1 | Writer 1 | P1 | Publisher 1 |
| W2 | Writer 2 | P2 | Publisher 2 |

Figure 5.2 Co-writer / co-publisher splits.

what you are about as a writer. If writing for film, Broadway, or commercials is a career goal, determine if the publisher is fluent and effective in these fields.

The fact that a publisher has made money in the past is not a guarantee of future performance. A publisher who has achieved great success may not be hungry enough to aggressively promote your songs. On the other hand, a young, untested publisher may not have the contacts to effectively promote and place a writers' works. Stylistic variety might be an impediment if you have a Nashville publisher, for example, who is simply not connected in the R&B business. On the other hand, if your publisher has offices in New York, Los Angeles, and Atlanta, they may be able to have their other offices promote your songs.

REALWORLD: **The Bell Curve**

To sign or not to sign. That is the question. There is no one-size-fits-all answer. Each and every long-term publishing offer, each and every single-song placement opportunity, has to be evaluated on its own merits. What may be reasonable in one situation may be abhorrent in another. Although the substantive and financial terms of the offer routinely determine whether a deal is acceptable, it has been our observation that the decision to enter into a publishing agreement—the acceptability of granting some portion of owned publishing rights to a third party—often follows the time-line of a Bell Curve. Notwithstanding the perennial advice to young writers and artists to seek the guidance of an entertainment attorney prior to signing any deal, the pull of exuberance, naiveté, and the need to jump-start a career often trumps caution and wisdom. Indeed, most beginning entertainment careers are littered with horror stories of bad decisions and bad deals: the flat part of a Bell Curve, signifying low resistance to offers. As writers and artists gain increased knowledge, advice, and confidence about their work, there is an increased tendency to scrutinize deals more closely, and retain more ownership: the higher part of the Bell Curve, signifying higher resistance to offers. Artists typically stay in this lofty portion of the curve . . . until they feel the pull of inactivity, age, or the need to re-jump-start their career with more "flexible" partnerships and deals. After years of low-level success, creators who still own "the whole loaf" begin to see a different wisdom in agreeing to enter into publishing deals which can serve to assist and propel their career: the backside, flat part of the Bell Curve, once again signifying a lower, more accommodating attitude towards offers. It is not unusual, in this regard, for some of the loudest proponents of "don't give away your publishing" in earlier stages of their career, becoming some of the strongest proponents and advocates of entering into publishing and co-publishing deals at a later stage of their career.

6 Independent songwriters

This chapter addresses those writers who choose to remain independent, and who choose to handle their own publishing activities. For every songwriter, there is always a fundamental career question about whether to enter into a publishing deal. As an independent writer, it becomes much more important to learn how to market and expose your songs, without the benefit of the expertise, clout, and financial resources of a publishing company. Owning the publishing rights to a song only becomes meaningful when someone is able to use that song to manage or create revenue.

Demo strategies for the singer-songwriter

The demo, essentially, should showcase exactly what you will be doing in a live performance. Three or four songs ought to be enough to get this across to the club owner. It is best, particularly in the early stages of a performing career, to severely limit your expenses in making a demo. Down the road you will be doing more elaborate recording projects. Home or garage studios can often be rented for a pittance, assuming you don't have one of your own. If you go to a professional studio, try to negotiate the price by trading a lower price for your willingness to record in the hours that the studio tends to be readily available. If a studio specializes in jingles, they are apt to have open time at night. If a studio concentrates on CD recording, they will be more apt to have the mornings vacant, because many artists don't like to sing in the morning.

If you are recording in a studio that doesn't possess very good equipment, you may want to rent a better studio for the final mix of your demo. By spending just a bit more money you will then have access to higher-quality equipment. Now it's time to look for more lucrative work in better venues.

Home studios vs. commercial studios

Whether a home studio is adequate for your demo depends upon the equipment that the studio has, and the production skills of the studio engineer. Remember you, the writer, are now paying for the demo, so if you are using a commercial studio, and hiring outside musicians, it's advisable to either have some notion of how to produce a song in the studio, or you need to hire someone who has production skills.

The commercial studio will generally have better outboard gear and echo chambers than the home studio possesses. It is also possible to find home studios that are operated by other song-writers. It is always a question of whether the product satisfies your goals. Sometimes recording in a small home or garage studio is not cost effective, because the engineer's skills are not really up to the task, and recording in a commercial studio might cost more by the hour, but less hours are used.

Keeping track of your business

If the songwriter is her own publisher, she needs to approach this task with the same dedication that a music publisher would utilize. This means that data bases need to be kept of when songs are submitted, who they are submitted to, and the date of the responses that an artist or producer makes to the song. Any calls made should be indicated, follow up calls need to be made, and there should be a paper trail of all of these activities. Any calls received must be quickly returned, or they may be too late for the caller's project. Demos must be cut, copies of the demos must be made, and the demos must be delivered quickly to appropriate listeners. Copyright notices must be filed, and lyric sheets or lead sheets duplicated. Acting as a publisher, the songwriter may wish to subscribe to Tip Sheets, to join NSAI and/or Taxi, to schedule open mic appearances and to attend seminars from the point of view of a publisher as well as a writer. When demos are sent out, the writer-publisher must be careful that contact names appear on the CD jewel box, on the lyric or lead sheet, and on any promotional material sent with the package. Appointments must be set with producers, record producers, and personal managers—anyone that can help to get the song recorded.

You are now in a position to decide whether you want to be your own music publisher, or whether you might be better off seeking a publishing or co-publishing deal with someone who is set up to fulfill all of the tasks, and has a staff that can do so. Certainly if you are going to have to do all of the things listed above, it will take away from your ability to spend time writing songs.

Although it is true that publishing your own material will double your royalty income, to quote the old industry cliché, 100 percent of nothing is nothing. Some musicians love the business as much as the music part of the music industry, but it is our experience the vast majority don't like doing the business, and aren't very good at it.

Getting songs recorded: pitching and shopping

It is helpful to package a lyric sheet when sending out demos. The writer should always include the name of her publishing company, in this case, her own company, and a copyright notice on the lyric sheet. Anything left with a record producer, artist, or record company should include contact information for the song. Placing all relevant contact information on the CD itself is critical. It is very likely that an interesting CD will get passed around from executive to executive, or will be listened to in an office and in a car. More often than not, the CD gets separated from the supporting bio and packaging, and the means to contact a songwriter is via contact information printed on the CD. It's not a good thing to have industry executives interested in a CD, and unable to contact the CD-owner.

A songwriter can utilize many of the same strategies that a music publisher does. He can read the tradepapers, such as *Billboard*, to keep up with the industry. *The Music Connection* has interviews with artists, songwriters, producers, and music publishers that may offer general or specific insights. It is possible, if the songwriter is willing to invest a few hundred dollars, to subscribe to Tip Sheets like *New on the Charts* that will keep the writer informed about new projects that artists are attempting, what kind of songs they are looking for, and who to send them to. *Music Row* is a Nashville tradepaper that includes many lists of artists who are recording, with the time line for their projects, and the specifics of what they are looking for.

The question that the songwriter needs to consider is whether the time spent promoting songs is useful, or whether the writer needs to leave that to other people, and spend her time writing the songs. In our experience, we have known a few writers who enjoy pitching songs and the process of convincing A&R people, artists, producers, and music supervisors to use their songs. The great majority of songwriters are not ideally suited for these roles, and do not enjoy undertaking them.

REALWORLD: **Psychology 101**

Pitching songs to industry executives requires a fine blend of art, skill, tenacity, ingenuity, luck, contacts, access, knowledge, credibility, timing, and, of course, having the right song. Although the right song seems to be of paramount importance, the other factors cannot be underestimated. Many of us were asked, in our college psychology classes, "are there more roses in the world because they are our favorite flower, or, are roses our favorite flower because there are so many of them?" [The answer, below.] This fundamental facet of human psychology is equally applicable to the world of music. A leading music executive is known to have a strong and close hand in selecting songs for her artists. Indeed, publishers have learned that obtaining a song approval and endorsement from the executive is nearly a guarantee that the song will be recorded by one of her many artists. And so, the executive becomes a key gatekeeper, through whom all songs must pass, and publishers dutifully send song demos for her consideration. It is also common practice that, after reviewing a song pitched by a publisher, the executive will simply write "pass, thanks" on the publisher's cover letter, and return the letter to the publisher. Very efficient and clear. But it is also common practice for co-publishers to separately send the same song demo to the executive on behalf of their own co-writer. And, as is the case with some very diligent publishers and writers, it is not unusual to send a revised demo of the same song—a second time. Two or three writers, two or three publishers, one or two demo versions . . . can result in the same song being sent to the executive numerous times. And as we all know from our own experience, the first time we heard some songs on the radio, they didn't really mean much to us. But after the third, or fourth (or tenth) time we heard the song, it started to grow on us. Call it human psychology, call it neuro-linguistic programming, or call it the psych 101 lesson learned about the number of roses in the world: "familiarity breeds preference." And, yes, our music executive is not exempt. After co-publishers received several "pass, thanks" letters from the executive about a specific song, we are aware of numerous times that she wrote the hallowed "great song, we'd like to record it" on the top of one of the publisher's letters, after having rejected the very same song several times before.

Leveraging your own contacts

Even if a songwriter has a publisher, the songwriter should work with the publisher to promote his songs. Sometimes an artist or a record producer is more open to hearing a song directly from the writer in an informal situation. You should not take the position that this is the publisher's job, because the fact is that the more recordings of your songs occur, the more money both of you will earn. Make a list of everyone that you know in the music industry. This should include road managers, musicians, singers, engineers, booking agents, managers, songwriters, record company and music publishing contacts, even stylists, industry organization employees, hairdressers, or music store employees. One of these people may be able to help you to access an artist or producer whose ears you are trying to capture with your songs. As an artist's career advances, the services of a personal manager may become necessary. The personal manager sees talent in terms of long-term career goals. In representing a singer-songwriter, the sorts of things that a manager looks at include:

- Does she write songs that could be commercially successful?
- Does she sing and perform well enough to secure a major record deal?

- Is her songwriting strong enough to attract interest for a publishing deal?
- Does she write for film or television, and are the songs possibly viable for use in commercials?

Placing collaborative songs

If you are collaborating with another writer, the two of you should pool each other's contacts to try to place a song. After you complete the song, if the two of you get together and start to list all of the possible artists who might record it, there is a reasonable chance that one of you knows a manager or a record producer working with a particular artist, or the artist herself, or her road manager. Other possible people in the chain might be anyone playing in the artist's band or singing backup for her, or the people doing sound for her, or even her road crew.

Building a singer-songwriter-performer career

Many singer-songwriters are increasingly turning to self-produced projects which are sold primarily at their own performances. Singer-songwriters, especially solo performers, often find rewarding performance outlets at coffeehouses and small venues. Today, most artists are releasing their own recordings. The Internet, and the advent of digital distribution "aggregators" (such as Ioda, InGrooves, and Big Fish Media)—companies that specialize in "distributing" (posting) CDs on the 40–50 digital music store sites—have become a significant means for promoting and selling independent music. And Internet "community" sites such as MySpace, YouTube, and FaceBook have also become very important elements of an independent artist's marketing and exposure campaign. More ambitious singer-songwriters hire regional or national independent promoters, who can assist in getting press and airplay, for a fee. Independent promoters, publicists, and public relations/marketing professionals, although very effective in promoting a career, can become very expensive, often costing $300.00–$500.00 per week for each service. CDs can be sold on consignment in local independent CD stores, many of which have local music sections, or the artist can seek to make a deal with an independent record distributor to get the recording into other markets.

Prior to getting radio airplay, most singer-songwriters who have independent deals or who own their own recordings, will sell the bulk of their product at personal appearances. Being able to generate a crowd, or playing at more popular venues will lead to selling more CDs.

REALWORLD: A digital strategy, by Bob Lefsetz

A more radical, digital strategy is expressed by attorney and author of the controversial newsletter, "The Lefsetz Letter."

How do you break a band? Word of mouth. Not via top-down carpet bombing. If something is good, everybody in the target demo is aware of it momentarily via txt, IM, old-fashioned email, pitchforkmedia.com, or stereogum or hypemachine or some music blog. Most people still find out about a band organically. Ever since the advent of over-hype, with MTV, band careers have become ever more brief. Only the oldsters, who developed organically, when you couldn't get on television on a regular basis, can tour a decade after they emerged, never mind three or four.

It is the Web's ability to create a brand at breakneck speed. Let's begin where everybody else does, MySpace. Once again, MySpace does not break acts. Most people never look at the homepage. What MySpace does is give you a place to listen to the music of acts. Usurping the need for a record company. For free, you can have your music hosted. Where not only "friends" can check it out, but professionals too. Viral Marketing: You can build a buzz. If you're good! Most bands on MySpace are bad. But now everybody expects every act to allow their music to be heard on MySpace! Were the major labels here first? No, they're begrudgingly following along. Terrestrial radio is still number one. But the savvy, the fans, they're constantly surfing and discovering. Which is why acts should have their music available in blogs, given away free everywhere! Because if the tastemakers have it, they can spread the word. You need a huge touring and radio presence. An act with a profile should be its own label.

© Bob Lefsetz, Music Industry Blogger, Lefsetz.com

Live performance, promotion, and exposure

Open mics

Open mics are evenings in clubs or coffeehouses where artists and/or writers get together and perform their songs in public, in a relaxed and informal setting. The most famous of these clubs is The Bluebird Café in Nashville, where the best writers in town get together and swap songs. Other versions of this event are taking place every week in cities all over the United States.

For someone trying to make a living as an artist, open mics are a mixed blessing, because they don't pay anyone to perform, except for the MC, but it's another opportunity to meet other writers, to get reactions from a generally supportive audience for your latest song, and to socialize with a group of people that share your interests. You don't have to be a great performer to play in these situations, because the emphasis is on songs rather than performances.

House concerts

During the last ten years, a live concert circuit has emerged, known as "house concerts." House concerts are exactly what they sound like: concerts held at the houses of people who enjoy hearing live music. They often take place in living rooms, but can also occur on patios, or on lawns, depending upon the physical situation of the house.

House concerts are a unique phenomenon in the sense that the presenters are simply people that love music. The presenter charges an admission fee, sometimes referred to as a donation. Many of the presenters do not take any money out of this charge, but give it all to the performer. Others take out a small amount of money for publicity and refreshments. A few presenters even tie the shows into catered meals, and deduct the cost of the meals from the overall receipts. Presenters also often offer free lodging to the performer or performers.

There are actually touring artists making a living by playing the house concert circuit full-time. The gigs come through word of mouth, and by doing Google searches. Throughout the United States and Europe, the presenters have essentially banded together and help performers go from one venue to the next.

House concerts have some unique characteristics. Since they

are being held in people's homes, the attendees are essentially invited guests. The preferred method of advertising these events is via email. Since the presenters don't want hundreds of people flocking to their homes, there is none of the postering or newspaper ads that performers are used to seeing. The performers in turn use their own email lists to inform people in the area that they will be performing.

Because the concerts are in intimate venues, and the audience is literally face to face with the performer, it is quite common to sell a large number of CDs to the audience, more than are sold in typical performances. The CD acts as a souvenir of a pleasant evening. Most performers add attendees to their mailing lists, and inform them of future performances in the area.

Because of the small venues, the performances are often done without a sound system. If the performer happens to have a small voice, this can be a hardship. It is also not a forum suitable for divas or narcissists. Because the setting is intimate, the performer should expect to spend time with the audience. If the performer has a strong need for privacy, this may also irritate the host. Some performers come in their own vans, outfitted for camping, and do not stay at the presenter's house. This should be worked out in advance, so that the presenter doesn't have hurt feelings. Since the "concert promoter" is not making any money from the event, it is important to have some regard for his feelings, if you intend to play more of these venues.

Many of the people who host house concerts prefer to have seen the performer in person to simply receiving a CD. Some are happy to get a video. Mostly they are looking to find performers who will have enough performance skills to relate to an audience that the presenter has invited into his own home. Since the presenters often network with other presenters, they will also take the word of other presenters that the performer will "put on a good show." It is a good idea to get letters of reference when you have done a successful house concert, especially if you do not have a video available.

Playing at clubs or coffeehouses

Open mic situations often occur in small clubs or coffeehouses. Nearly every town now has a free cultural/events newspaper which lists such venues. The daily newspaper also often lists these places in their Friday or Sunday entertainment section. If you can't find such information in your town, check with other songwriters, songwriting organizations or performers.

As a performer, initially you should expect to perform for little or no money. The point of performing is to gain experience. You need to become comfortable in front of a live audience, and you need to learn to present the part of your personality that people will find intriguing or attractive. You should also attend other shows, and watch the way performers relate to the audience. You will quickly ascertain what sort of performances work, and the kind of attitude or presentation that tends to make an audience feel uncomfortable. Some performers trade on charm, some on humor, some on good looks, some possess some indefinable but appealing quality, and some combine all of these abilities.

The next step is probably the most difficult in the life of the aspiring artist. When do you start charging money for your services, and how much do you charge? If you have been performing with some regularity at particular venues, and have been receiving positive audience response, it is time to talk to the owner of the venue, or to seek out other venues where you think your music would work, and to approach the owner or manager about getting a paid gig in her club or coffeehouse. Initially it makes little difference as to how much money you will make. It is more about the principle of the thing: you are now a professional and you need to charge for your services. The amount that you charge should be based on a realistic appraisal of the size of the venue, the price of the food, coffee, or alcohol served, and the number of people that you feel you can draw.

Naturally some of this is hypothetical, because until you start to play as the featured act, you can't possibly know how many people you will draw. Different venues follow different customs. Some will slap a cover charge on attendees, and they will simply give the performer that income, reserving the profits from selling food or drink for the club. Other clubs will pay a percentage of the bar receipts, and still others will simply pay you a salary, and hope that you will draw enough people to justify that expense.

Industry showcases

In the major music industry towns, sometimes an artist will arrange for a club to hold a special performance for music industry people. The artist and/or his manager will invite record company presidents, A&R people, music publishers, or anyone that they know in the business. These events can be very exciting, particularly if there is an industry buzz about the artist. We have seen such events turn into music industry bidding wars, when it appears obvious that a particular performer has those magical and intangible qualities that convince professionals that they are witnessing the birth of an important career. Industry buzz is created through word of mouth, reviews, hype by managers and publicists, and believe it or not, sometimes by undeniable talent.

Publicity and advertising

Some clubs regularly advertise in newspapers or even on the radio. Others put together flyers that list their events for an entire month. You will need to supply the venue with some color photos, and some promotional material. Promotional material means a brief biography, particularly about any of your musical achievements, along with anything that will arouse interest or get attention from either media people or the general reader. No one cares about your junior high trombone lessons, but people will be intrigued that you set the state record for the 400 meter run. If you have received any positive reviews from local newspapers or magazines, you should mention them in your bio. It is also a good idea to have your bio, a photo in PDF form, and some MP3s available for a complete electronic press kit (EPK). This can be delivered to clubs or to media people in a matter of minutes, and doesn't require you to spend money on postage. You should talk to the operator of the venue to find out whether she will be doing any PR or advertising. If not, you should send notices to daily and weekly newspapers, as well as any of the numerous monthly publications and Internet options that have emerged in recent years. Many cities also have slick monthly magazines that print entertainment listings, and others have music and entertainment guides. You may also want to print up flyers and post them around town, especially in locations in the immediate vicinity of the club.

Where you live

An important consideration that an aspiring writer-publisher may face is the question of where he lives. Although this decision has been significantly minimized by the advent of the Internet, digital distribution, viral promotion, and strong regional music scenes, there is no question that close access to industry executives and a vibrant creative community can greatly advance a career. If a writer intends to write music for film and television, or chooses to compose film scores, the major media markets in New York and Los Angeles clearly present much greater opportunities. Technology, however, has greatly assisted the long-distance composer. Real-time remote recording sessions, FTP sites, and MP3 submissions have allowed non-local writers and composers to effectively submit material, and compete with local writers. *The Songwriter's Market* (TSM), published annually, is an excellent resource for songwriters seeking information about publishers and record company activities. TSM includes the names and addresses of record companies, producers, and music publishers and the sorts of music and projects that they are involved in. It also indicates whether or not a company accepts unsolicited material. The key factor, however, remains the nature of the relationship that a writer has with the executive and creative community. We conclude that for the fanatically ambitious singer-songwriter, being on the scene, being able to contact artists, producers, musical supervisors, and the other members of the music industry infrastructure is a necessity.

No matter where a writer or artist lives, it is a good idea to visit the places where the music industry is active. A primary goal is simply to make contacts, and to grasp how the industry operates, and what the industry wants. Make your trip to the city in conjunction with a major music industry event, such as the Nashville Songwriters Association International (NSAI) seminars, or the ASCAP Songwriters Expo, in Los Angeles. These events provide excellent opportunities to hear and learn, first hand, how record producers, artists, and music publishers talk about the music industry. There are music conferences in many large cities, and the prominent music organizations and Performing Rights Organizations in the United States and Canada have substantial website resources outlining the nature and locations of these events.

7 Music in film and television

Film and television music

Music in the movies is an essential element of the filmmaking process and is often a significant factor that contributes to box office success. Throughout the world, there are thousands of major and independent film and television productions each year which create income opportunities for composers and songwriters. Films typically are released in motion picture theaters, but they create significant subsequent ancillary revenue streams for their producers and the attached songwriters, composers, and publishers, when they are made commercially available as DVDs, and when they are exhibited on global, free, network, satellite, cable, and pay television outlets. Royalties from the sales of songs and scores which are included on soundtrack albums, digital download or streaming sites, and commercial advertising campaigns also generate license income and royalties for creators and publishers.

There are two primary rights involved in the use of music in a film or television show, each generating so-called "front-end" fees: (1) the synchronization right, which compensates the writer and publisher for the use of their *composition* in a visual production; and (2) the Master Recording Right, which compensates the owner of that specific *recording* of the composition. The Master Rights are typically owned by a record label, and those rights must be acquired through negotiation with the record company; and the composition rights are owned by the publisher and writer, and must be acquired through negotiation with the publisher (and on behalf of the writer). The "synch" and "Master" fees can be substantial, as we will see below. When a producer feels that he may not need a specific "hit" recording of a song for the film, he has the option to license a less-well-known, less-expensive version of the song, and therefore may avoid paying the Master License fees which could be charged by the label. The fees for the license and use of the underlying copyrighted composition, however, cannot be avoided. When a producer needs a specific song, he must negotiate with the publisher of that song. The writer and publisher, therefore, enjoy unique revenue and royalty streams which are often-times unavailable to the record companies. Small record companies will often offer tracks at lower license fees in exchange for the exposure that the production may provide for the artist. Similarly, composers who control their own publishing will often allow their songs to be used for lower fees for the same reason.

"Front-end" fees / "back-end" fees

Synchronization licenses

Synchronization rights are those rights which allow a film or television producer to use ("synchronize") songs or a score with a visual motion picture. The "synch fees" are totally negotiable between the music publisher and the producer of a film or television show. These fees, as well, vary according to the stature of the artist, and the relation of the specific recording to the film. The synch fee is negotiated by the publisher with the licensee (music user), and the license fee depends on a number of factors, such as: (1) the timing and use of the song in the production; (2) the overall budget of the production; (3) the stature of the copyright (i.e., whether the song is a hit or relatively unknown); (4) the rights the licensing party is seeking, that is, term (one year, five years, perpetuity), territory (United States, Europe, world), the media for exploitation (home video/DVD, TV, theatrical, Internet, etc.). In the current practice in licensing songs for film and television, the producer generally seeks to negotiate a license for all known and future media, and they prefer to license the song in perpetuity. Should the movie or television show prove to be a massive success, you may regret granting such a license for a relatively low fee as the show is repeatedly broadcast worldwide on cable television. On the other hand, the publisher and songwriter can console themselves through the extensive amount of performance royalty income that the show generates. The publisher may also attempt to restrict the number of years that the song may be utilized, and to create a series of annual options, so that if the song continues to be used, each year the synchronization fee will escalate. It all depends on the value of the song, the strength of the music publisher, and the eagerness that a producer or director may have to use a particular song. Clearly certain songs may provide a perfect fit with a specific plot line or mood.

The motion picture synchronization fee paid to the music publisher (which is shared with the songwriter) for the use of a song can include the right to distribute the film to network, local, syndicated, pay-per-view, pay, satellite, cable, and subscription television stations; the right to show the film in motion picture theaters in the United States; and the right to include the song in trailers, previews, and advertisements of the motion picture. Each of these elements is a separate and distinct negotiable right. Foreign theatrical distribution rights (i.e. the right to show a film in motion picture theaters outside the United States) are also given to the producer, but such rights are subject to the payment of performance fees by theaters to the various Performing Rights Organizations in countries outside the United States. If the title of an opening credit song is also used as the title of the film (but the film's plot is not based on the story line of the song) the fees are increased further (e.g. from $75,000 to over $500,000).

Valuing music: how uses of music affect the license fee

There are several key factors that publishers consider in determining how much to charge for the use of a song in a film. The key factors that will determine the license fee that a publisher will seek include:

- Was the song written or recorded by a major artist or writer?
- What is the budget of the film, and what is the budget for the music portion of the film?
- What is the history/popularity/stature of the song?
- How is the song being used in the production?
- Does the subject matter of the film derive from the lyric of the song?
- Is the title of the song used as the title of the film?
- What is the term of the proposed use?
- What territory is covered by the license?

- What is the intended distribution, exhibition, and marketing/ sales plan for the film?
- Are ancillary uses of the song anticipated (DVDs, Internet, mobile, satellite)?

If a song has been recorded by a major artist, presumably there will be a recognition factor for the viewer, and that should increase the value of the song. If a song has been a hit more than once, and especially if the performances have been musically different, the recognition factor will increase. The question of how a song is being used relates to such matters as whether the song is being played in the foreground as part of the action, or is barely audible on a car radio while the action is focused on an entirely different matter. If the usage is only a ten-second snippet of the song, as opposed to a complete performance, that will clearly reduce the fee. The synchronization fees charged by music publishers for major studio films are usually between $10,000.00 and $50,000.00, but can vary widely based on several factors, below. It should also be mentioned that record companies normally charge between $10,000.00 and $40,000.00 for the use of existing Master Recordings in a major studio film. Songs used at the beginning or end of a film or television show are considered to be more important to that show. The song used at the beginning may set the scene for the entire plot, while a song at the end can be essentially a summary of the film.

REALWORLD: **The golden goose**

Notwithstanding the guidelines, above, used to determine an appropriate front-end synch license fee, there is a fine art and balance to be weighed in assessing the value of potential back-end performance income that may be generated via a synch placement. Once a license and synch fee have been agreed to, there is no certainty as to how a song will be used and cut into the final production (background, visual vocal, etc.), and there is no certainty as to how many seconds or minutes of the song will be used. And there surely is no assurance of how often the production will be performed. Each of these factors contributes significantly to the amount of back-end performance income that the song will generate. It is reasonable to assume, therefore, that a composer would be more inclined to accept a smaller front-end synch fee, if it were clear that the back-end performance income was assured. Conversely, if the potential back-end performance income appeared to be limited (the production was to be aired only once on a small cable outlet, for example), the writer and publisher may be justified in seeking a larger front-end synch fee. Although this analysis works in theory, it is very hard to put into practice. An emerging writer was offered a synch placement in a new television series. Although the show was receiving positive reviews, there was certainly no guarantee that the production would go into broad domestic syndication, or that it would be distributed in any of the potentially lucrative foreign markets. The Music Supervisor, claiming a "very tight first-year music budget," offered a decidedly low synch fee to the young writer. The writer's publisher declined the synch offer, stating that the license fee was "considerably lower than industry standard" for such a use. The writer, however, was not as concerned with the financial rewards of the placement as she was with the publicity and credits that she could tout on her website and in her press kit. After considerable discussion, and the strong persuasion of the writer, the publisher agreed to accept the unusually small synch fee. The use of the song, as it turns out, was a featured performance, lasting nearly two minutes in duration. The back-end performance income was considerable—for writer and publisher—and the show continues to be seen in syndication, generating additional performance income. The decision to accept a lower synch fee, in this case, was a wise decision. Synchronization offers, however, should not be considered lightly. It is important to weigh the financial—as well as non-financial—benefits that accrue to writers who have music used in film and television. As creators, writers (and their publishers) seek to protect and maintain the high value of their craft, and rightly tend to reject synch offers based on a small front-end fee. But accepting some lower synch fees does start to build a catalogue of performed works, and allows for the chance of growing significant back-end royalties.

Music supervisors

The traditional Hollywood movie score, circa 1930–70, consisted of many minutes of instrumental music, together with one or two songs. Over the years, it became apparent that if a movie included a hit song, this would serve the function of inducing more people to see the movie, and in turn the movie would cause people to purchase the recording of the song. The studios began to realize that if they could include a dozen important songs in a movie they could reduce the need for instrumental music, and they would be able to attract a younger audience to see their films. The use of multiple songs did not necessarily save money, because there was a trade-off between paying for synchronization rights for a dozen songs, against using a large orchestra and having to pay musicians' union rates for playing. However, songs were a more predictable commodity, because when new instrumental music was commissioned, the director and producer were never entirely sure what they would be getting. Since the songs were usually taken from existing recordings, they could be played against picture while the movie was being produced.

To meet this emerging new need for selecting and licensing songs, producers and directors sought the services of a sophisticated executive with broad song expertise: the music supervisor. The job of the supervisor is to propose songs to the director and producer of the movie, and when the songs are approved, to work out the financial details with the music publisher, and, if the original recording is used, with the recording company for that portion of the rights. A good music supervisor has an encyclopedic knowledge of music, and a passion for musical research. In many ways the role of the music supervisor is analogous to what an A&R person does at a record company. As there is an ever-growing sophistication of the role of music in films and in television, the role of talented music supervisors has become increasingly important.

Music casting

Music "casting" for film and television parallels actor casting: the process involves considering, evaluating, and selecting the right song or score for a particular scene. Music supervisors, in coordinating the music needed for a production, will typically send publishers a synopsis or description of the scene, dialogue, and action at the time the music will be placed. The scene synopsis gives the publisher and writer the chance to consider how their music will be used, and how to properly quote a license fee for the usage. A publisher may also have certain restrictions in its agreement with the songwriter which require additional approvals from the songwriter. The Master Recording owner is provided the same scene description information, for the very same reasons. Although placing music in films is often-times rushed towards the final weeks of editing, the timeframes and deadlines for placing music in television productions are significantly more hectic. Weekly television series, shot on a seven-day schedule, may not even be packaged, edited, and ready to dub in final music cues until the night prior to broadcast.

REALWORLD: Scene descriptions

In the sometimes hectic rush to get music placed into television programs, publishers may not always receive complete scene descriptions, or have enough time to fully evaluate the nuances of the use of their music in the production. A network Top Ten television program recently called publishers, seeking "to replace a major female recording artist's song that would be playing on the car radio in which the stars of the program were riding." This was the entire written scene description, sent by fax, to some key publishers. The producers were dubbing the replacement song into the show the next morning: a very quick song approval was necessary. Conventional wisdom suggests that the major female recording artist's label and publisher sought too much money for the use of the song, requiring the show's producers to find more affordable replacement music that "sounds like" pop music. Emerging writer-artists, when given the chance to have their music used in a Top Ten television program, generally jump at the chance. Not only will there be front-end synch and Master Recording fees, as well as back-end public performance royalties, but these kinds of television placements go a long way in building a reputation and exposure for the artist. And so, the writer-artist eagerly granted the approval for use of her song as the "car radio" song, and organized a TV-watching party for all of her friends for the air date. A week later, as the show was broadcast, the writer's friends, along with the rest of the country, watched intently as the scene developed, and the stars of the show left their apartment to go for a car ride. Moments into the car ride, one of the stars asks for the radio to be turned on, and our young writer's song is played through the car speakers! A rare and special moment in any writer's life, eagerly shared with friends and strangers around the country. And ten seconds into the song, one of the stars in the car says "oh no, not her again," and proceeds to stick her finger in her throat, feigning disgust with the theoretical "major artist," and changes the channel.

The scene description was accurate, but only to a point. Did the major female recording artist really turn down the placement because the fee was too low, or was she provided with a more complete scene description? And ultimately, was this a beneficial use and placement for the young writer-artist, or a bad career move? Although the actual use of the song was not positive, the writer-artist felt that she (1) received substantial fees, (2) was able to promote the TV-use of her music on her website and bio, and (3) since no-one ever knew who the "radio artist" really was, suffered no negative impact on her writing career.

Remember that performing rights do not apply to films shown in U.S. movie theaters, but are very much a factor in television shows, or when a film is shown on television. Television producers will often try to limit synchronization payments by telling the publisher that public performance payments "on the back end"—when the show is broadcast on television and surveyed by a Performing Rights Organization—will make up for small "front-end" licensing payments. Of course the producer cannot guarantee exactly how many times the show will be broadcast, or whether it will then be sold to cable, and to television stations in other parts of the world. If the show is well known and is currently broadcast on network television, the publisher and songwriter can rest assured that the song will generate additional "back-end" performance royalties as a result of repeated domestic (and foreign) showings of the show.

The budgets for television shows are generally lower than the budgets for films. According to Jeffrey and Todd Brabec's authoritative book, *Music, Money And Success: the Insider's Guide to Making Money in the Music Business*, synchronization fees for a song used on a network television show range from $1,750.00 to $3,500.00 for a one-to-five year license (once again split 50–50 between the publisher and the songwriter). As a greater number of musicians are now able to produce quality-sounding recordings at home, there are an increasing number of tracks being submitted to film and television music supervisors. What used to be the domain of a relatively limited number of record companies, publishers, and music libraries, the world of pitching music to film and television has now grown to include independent artists, home-grown producers, and innovative songpluggers. With the increased availability of quality recordings, the supply-side of the equation has begun to lower the demand-side fees that producers will now pay for synch licenses.

Just as movies may spawn hit songs, television shows have also produced hit songs and major recording artists. *The Sopranos* theme song, A3's "Woke Up This Morning," has enjoyed enormous success, based on its impact and presence on the HBO show. "Woke Up This Morning" does what all great theme songs should do: generates anticipation, immediately puts the viewer in a focused frame of mind, and creates the kind of sonic familiarity that breeds audience loyalty. Today, record companies (and some of the production companies, themselves) are releasing CDs featuring songs and artists that have been used on their shows, much like movie soundtrack albums.

REALWORLD: **Rock star**

Bert, the principal writer in a rock band, relocated to Los Angeles, in hopes of securing a major label recording contract. The band played the usual clubs, and had gathered a modest following, in hopes of gaining industry attention, or better yet, industry "buzz." Attempts at getting signed, after a few years, proved fruitless. The band, nonetheless, kept at it—pitching their tapes and doing showcases, wherever possible. To no avail. Notwithstanding good songwriting, persistent performing, and continued efforts to attract major label interest, the band did not get signed, and eventually broke up. The songs, however, continued to circulate among industry executives. One of the band's tapes eventually made its way to the person in charge of coordinating music for a television project (the "music supervisor"). The music supervisor was looking for background music and a theme song, for a television show in development. One of Bert's songs caught the ear of the supervisor, who thought the song captured both the lyrical and emotional essence of the show. Following the intense internal process (and competition) of evaluating songs for use as a theme song for a television pilot, Bert's song was eventually selected as the theme song for the show. The television show, with Bert's theme song, became a substantial hit, and later went into broad syndication. Because of its popularity, the television series was also produced as a retail DVD product, which enjoys on-going sales success. Bert received (1) a synchronization fee for allowing his song to be used with the visual production, (2) substantial on-going songwriter performance rights royalties during the show's lengthy network run, (3) substantial on-going songwriter performance rights royalties during the show's lengthy syndication run, (4) mechanical royalties for the right to include his song in the sales of DVDs of the show, and (5) artist and writer royalties from the sales of CDs of Bert's resurrected band playing the "hit TV theme." Notwithstanding the "failure" of Bert's band to get a recording contract, Bert-the-songwriter has enjoyed a very lucrative career.

Instrumental music

A typical music budget in a film is roughly 3–5 percent of the budget for the entire project. If a film is budgeted at $30 million, the music budget may be roughly $900,000.00–$1,500,000.00. Music budgets can vary significantly, depending on the preference of the director, the role that music will play in the film, and the stature of the artists and composer that the director wants to include in the soundtrack.

Many films employ a well-known composer and a large

orchestra. Composer fees vary wildly, depending on the reputation of the composer, and on how committed the producer and director are to making music an important part of the project.

While composers and publishers do not receive public performance royalties from films shown in U.S. theaters, they do receive performance royalties when the film is shown in foreign markets, when the film is shown on television, and when the songs or score from the film are included in a soundtrack CD. Sometimes a music publisher will reduce the amount of a synchronization fee in exchange for a guarantee that a song will be placed on a soundtrack album.

There are hundreds of independent film makers around the country who also need to have music for their films. Often these films are made with small budgets. Emerging film composers need to be very innovative in their deal-making to obtain scoring jobs. Clearly, one good score may lead to another. As is the case in negotiating synch fees for the license of a particular song, film composers must weigh the balance between (1) front-end fees, (2) back-end performance income, and (3) the credit and experience of writing a film score. Step Deals, wherein benchmark additional fees are paid to the composer as the film becomes more successful, are an excellent way of negotiating for fair up-side compensation, without creating a financial burden for the independent producer at the outset of her production.

Soundtrack albums

Music publishers, in negotiation with a producer, may agree to accept a reduced synchronization fee for a song if the producer guarantees that the song will be on a soundtrack album released by a major label. Sometimes there are even guarantees of an "A" side single release, but these usually occur only when a successful recording artist on a major label records the song for the film. In this case, the publisher may give two price quotes: a higher figure if the song does not make the soundtrack album or if an album is not released and, because of the possibility of additional ancillary album income, a lower quote if the soundtrack provision actually takes effect. For example, if a publisher gives a $25,000.00 quote for the use of a song in a film, it also might agree to reduce the price to $22,000.00 if there is a guarantee of a nationally distributed soundtrack album, and may even further reduce the fee if the song becomes an "A" side single from the album. In virtually all instances where the writer is a recording artist, the terms of the soundtrack album will also be negotiated, including artist/producer royalties and mechanical licensing arrangements. In some cases, the film company will provide the writer with a demo budget so that the producer will be able to hear the newly created composition with further payments due upon delivery of the final composition to the film company, and inclusion in the motion picture. For example, the film company might pay the writer to produce a demo recording and make an additional payment upon completion of the composition and another payment if the composition is actually put in the motion picture.

REALWORLD: "Who's zoomin' who?"

The film industry, in routinely producing thirty and forty million dollar pictures, is clearly known to be the bigger dog at the music-film water cooler. After all, a CD can be produced for a few hundred thousand dollars, and can only generate a fraction of what a successful film generates. It's not unusual for studios, after spending $40 million to produce and market a film, to invest another few hundred thousand dollars in a soundtrack CD, as an additional means of promotion, support, and exposure for the picture. A radio hit, closely aligned with a film, can contribute significantly to continued box office success for a picture ("My Heart Will Go On" in *Titanic*). The few hundred thousand dollar investment in the CD can prove to be a very wise marketing tool for the film. The songwriter-publisher-artist community sees it a little differently: we license a song to a soundtrack CD, and look at the $30 or $40 million that the film studio has spent as an additional means of promotion and exposure for the song.

Trailers

Trailers are the short commercials and promotional advertisements, seen on television and in movie theaters, which are used to promote a movie. Trailers can use music that is already a part of the production, or the producer may choose to use new, unrelated music, which is not included in the project, for the advertising campaign. Fees for the use of a song in a trailer typically are in the $5,000.00–$20,000.00 range, and an equal Most Favored Nations (MFN) Master License fee is generally also paid to acquire the rights to use the recording of the song. When a song is used in the film, the synchronization license usually grants the producer the right to use the song in promotional theatrical trailers, as well as in television and radio advertisements.

Work-for-hire agreements

Nearly all film and studio composer agreements are work-for-hire agreements. Under a work-for-hire contract, the producer/studio negotiates to become the publisher of a composition or score, pursuant to an agreement with the composer. In "for-hire" agreements, the composer retains the "writer share" of all of the music composed for the production, and the publishing share of the work is retained by the studio or production company. The composer typically grants to the producer/studio "all rights, title, and interest throughout the world in perpetuity, in and to the work and the publishing share and the ownership of the recordings." By operation of this grant from the composer, the producer becomes the owner of the worldwide copyright in the composition for the entire duration of copyright protection. The work-for-hire clause is typically broad, and seeks to transfer all copyright and other rights "throughout the entire universe now known or hereinafter created." The copyright act states:

A "work made for hire" is—

(1) a work prepared by an employee within the scope of his or her employment; or

(2) a work specially ordered or commissioned for use as a contribution to a collective work, as a part of a motion picture or other audiovisual work, as a translation, as a supplementary work, as a compilation . . . if the parties expressly agree in a written instrument signed by them that the work shall be considered a work made for hire.

Under (1) above, the creator must be an actual employee at the time the work was created, or, under (2), a person who is not an employee but an independent contractor can still fall within the work made for hire concept, but only if the work has been specially ordered or commissioned and only if the parties have executed a written agreement declaring a work made for hire contract.

8 Music in advertising and Production Music Libraries

Advertising music

Most of the major television and radio commercials evolve as a result of a product manufacturer and an advertising agency getting together to develop a marketing concept for a new campaign. The ad agency solicits various independent music houses to submit demos based on the concept. Sometimes a copy writer at the agency has written the lyric. In other instances, they simply have a number of phases or product keys that they want the composer to insert into the lyric. As is the case with film composers and their studio contracts, most ad agencies employ "work-for-hire" agreements in their contracts with composers. In much the same way that studios seek to own and control the songs that are used in their productions, ad agencies—or the companies which manufacture the product being advertised—seek to control how the songs identified with their products will be licensed in the future. In addition to controlling future uses of the song, work-for-hire owners are quite aware that they will earn the public performance royalties, as publishers, from airplay. For the composer and the work-for-hire owner/publisher, even though advertising royalties are a fraction of what radio songs earn, popular commercials and infomercials can air repeatedly, and generate significant income.

Before the proliferation of sophisticated and affordable home studios, there used to be a thriving business in producing and recording demos for commercials. The demos were done in studios, and the musicians were always paid the union scale for recording, which is approximately $100.00 an hour, with a one hour minimum call. Sometimes the singers were paid, and some-times they did the sessions on "spec," waiving initial fees in hopes that if the demo led to a final session, the singers were apt to see substantial recording and back-end artist royalties. Today most of the independent music houses have their own studios, and the demos are generally done free. Often few if any musicians are used, because the parts are played on synthesizers and drum machines. Another jingle composer ploy is that a jingle may consist of a recording performed entirely on synthesizers. There is a near-legendary story of one such jingle done in New York, where the composer played twenty-six different parts on synthesizers, and put his name on the union contract twenty-six times. He used the reasoning that essentially he was playing twenty-six different instrumental parts. Looking at it another way, he was replacing twenty-five other musicians on the session.

Licensing songs for commercials

Certain songs and recording artists convey images that seem to mesh perfectly with specific products. In Jim Webb's excellent book *Inside the Art of Songwriting*, he mentions that some years after the deal had been made for TWA to use his song *Up, Up and Away* as a commercial, he heard the song being broadcast on late night radio. He was unaware that they had begun to use the song again after a lapse of some years. It turned out that they owed him thousands and thousands of dollars under his agreement with the advertising agency. Webb (and the authors and our readers) wondered if, had he not had insomnia that night, he would ever have received the money due him. The moral of the story is that a songwriter and a music publisher always need to be tuned in to current uses even of their older works.

There are no set fees for these uses. Fees are negotiated between the advertising agency and the music publisher. Fees can run as high as a million dollars. As usual, it depends upon the value of the song, whether the use is local, regional, or national, if it is used on radio as well as television, and so on. There is usually an option that requires the agency to increase the payment if, for example, the commercial is run for an additional year. Currently some alternative rock bands have used commercials primarily for exposing themselves on a national basis, rather than focusing on making large amounts of money from them. Certain artists have refused to let their songs be licensed for commercials, because they regarded commercials as a sell-out of their musical principles. If you are a songwriter or composer and do not want your material used in commercials, attempt to have an approval clause inserted in your publishing contract that states that the publisher cannot use your songs in specified situations, without your permission.

Production Music Libraries

"Production Music" is produced, owned, or represented by collectives of composers, producers, or agents who typically compile broad catalogues—Production Music Libraries—of unsigned, unreleased commercial music, which is then licensed to customers for use in film, television, radio, commercials, and other media.

Unlike popular and classical music publishers, who typically own 50 percent (co-publishing) of the copyright in a composition, Production Music Libraries own all of the copyrights of their music, usually through negotiating work-for-hire agreements with their composers. This allows for licensing the works without seeking the composer's permission, as may be necessary in licensing music from traditional publishers. Libraries also acquire the rights from the composer/producer/label to represent the Master Recording rights of the track. Production Music Libraries, therefore, are a very convenient source of material for producers—as they can license rights to both the composition and the recording as a "one-stop" music provider. License fees charged by libraries are typically lower than the fees charged by traditional publishers and major labels.

Production Music Libraries will typically offer a broad range of musical styles and genres, enabling producers and editors to find much of what they need in the same library. Music libraries vary in size from a few hundred tracks up to several thousand. Libraries typically enjoy reputations for having either a broad, diverse catalogue of high-quality audio recordings, or having a smaller catalogue of unique, artist-oriented bands. The buyer (licensee) makes a decision on the type of music that will work best for her production and her target audience.

Music libraries are based on two income streams. (1) Front-end license (synchronization) fees are paid upfront to the library for permission to synchronize its music to a piece of film, video, or audio. These fees can range from a few dollars for an Internet usage, to thousands of dollars for a network or commercial advertising use. Some libraries, depending on the negotiation, split the synch fees with the composer of the music. It is also common for a composer to be paid a work-for-hire fee upfront by the library for composing the music, effectively selling the Master Rights to her share of license fees. (2) Back-end performance royalties are generated when library music is publicly performed. Typically, a library will receive 50 percent of the performance income as publisher from their PRO, with the composer receiving the remaining 50 percent, as writer. Just as front-end license fees are variable and entirely negotiable, performance income is highly variable and dependent on the nature and frequency of the music usage.

"Royalty-free" libraries

With the proliferation of music libraries in recent years and the subsequent increase in competition, some smaller libraries have created the "royalty-free" model. These libraries may not charge their customers for licensing the music. Instead, the customers can purchase the rights to use a bundle of CDs—with the price based on the number of CDs and the type of music needed— whose content is licensed in perpetuity for the customer to use as often as he wishes. These libraries depend mainly on back-end performance royalties for their income. Since royalty-free music deprives composers and libraries of a significant source of income, libraries employing this model typically cannot attract the level of talent and quality that their traditional-model counterparts do, and royalty-free libraries are generally seen as a cheaper option for those on a limited budget. Historically, Production Music's reputation has suffered from a perceived lack of quality. In truth, most of the music owned by the top libraries in the business is of entirely professional quality, and will often use veteran composers, engineers, and performers. At the lower end of the market, standards of production and composition tend to be more variable.

Needle-drop music

When an advertising agency or a producer needs music and has a very low budget, they resort to a needle-drop arrangement with Music Production Libraries. These libraries have hundreds of instrumentals and songs that can be plugged into commercials and films at a very low cost, often $5.00–$100.00 per segment used.

These uses are referred to as "needle drops." The music production houses have become more sophisticated over the years, as synthesizers, samplers, drum machines, and home studios have proliferated. The libraries generally use generic classifications, such as "up-tempo fiddle tunes." A film editor or someone doing a commercial can simply plug in the desired mood to their project. The selections tend to be very generic, because the have not been composed for use in a specific project, but simply provide general moods.

They also often sound familiar, because many people have already used a particular track. Many recording studios have these music libraries, and clients can use whatever they need. The studio then pays the music library their fee. Some of the music libraries have large orchestral compositions, often recorded outside the United States, where musicians are willing to work at rates lower than those in the major U.S. music cities.

Music library composers often play all of their own instrumental parts by using samplers. Singers, musicians, and composers all receive only a single payment and no re-use fees, and the work is often done without union contracts. Libraries utilize staff composers who are on salary, or who own a share of the company. A similar business exists for radio stations' IDs. These are packages that are generally sold to a radio station with the provision that a similar package will not be sold in the same metropolitan area. The same instrumental beds are often used for different stations in different cities.

9 Classical music, Broadway, print music, and educational music

Classical music

Classical, or "serious" music, as it is often called, is a very different genre and market from the pop music business. When a symphony orchestra plays a symphonic work, it must rent the parts for up to 105 musicians, depending upon the size of the orchestra. The two primary publishers of classical music in the United States are Theodore Presser, distributed by Hal Leonard, and G. Schirmer, distributed by Music Sales. These companies also distribute the music of many European music print publishers. Similar conditions prevail for opera performances and chamber music recitals.

As with all other print music contracts, the royalties are paid to the music publisher, who then distributes the income to the composer. Some of the younger classical composers arc handling the rights to their own music. The rental fees paid for classical music scores vary from a few hundred dollars to thousands of dollars. It depends upon whether a particular work is very popular at the present time or if it has never been performed before. Some opportunities for classical music composers are not obtained through music publishers. Grants are available from various organizations, and some successful musicians or musical groups commission works from composers.

Commissions for composers

Earlier in the book, we mentioned the commissioning of musical works in the world of classical music. There are two sorts of commissions that may occur. One is when a composer wins a contest which carries a prize of commissioning a new work that will be played by a professional orchestra. In many instances it is the orchestra that has commissioned the work. Another possible commission comes from a performing group that is looking to perform new works. The Kronos Quartet, in particular, is a string quartet that has gone out of its way to commission new works. When a work is commissioned, the artist financing the work expects to do the first performance of the work. This often leads to his recording the work. Although classical music rarely sells quantities of records, remember that the mechanical rights are 1.75 cents a minute for songs longer than five minutes, so a ten-minute piece will generate a royalty of 17.5 cents, as compared to the typical 9.1 cents that most songs receive. If a work becomes popular, the artist may very well add it to his normal concert schedule, where once again the piece will earn performance royalties. The best of all outcomes occurs when an artist records the work, continues to perform it, and other artists hear it and choose to add it to their own repertoire.

Broadway and Grand Rights

The rights to use songs in theatrical productions fall under a different category to any other copyright. They are referred to as "Grand Rights." Grand Rights involve three different creative areas: the person who writes the book or the written plot of a play, the composer, and the lyricist.

Songs used in Broadway or theatrical productions are licensed differently than songs used in typical radio or television. Grand Rights refers to the dramatic rights in a musical composition, which usually are important in a Broadway show or even a motion picture where music is being used to advance the drama. Those rights are separate and distinct from "small performance rights," which are the traditional performing rights, which accrue when a composition is publicly performed or broadcast. Performing Rights Societies are granted the right to administer small performance rights on behalf of their writer and publisher members, but Grand Rights are negotiated and administered by the original publisher, or its designated Grand Rights administrator.

The royalties for Broadway musicals are governed by the Dramatists Guild. The Guild codes cover the period when a producer initially options the show, the run of the show itself, touring productions, productions by local dinner theaters, and regional theater companies. Once a show has opened, a minimum royalty of 4.5 percent is paid on gross box office receipts, split among the three creative roles, and after the show has recouped its expenses, the royalty increases to 6 percent. The royalties can also be distributed through "pooling" the profits of the show, and dividing it not only between the three creative contributors, but also among a number of other people involved in the show, including choreographers and lighting designers. During the run of the show, the songwriters and the author of the book are guaranteed a minimum weekly payment, even if the show is not breaking even.

Of course, significant royalties can be earned when a show has a long run, and spawns road companies. An Andrew Lloyd Webber production, with multiple shows running on Broadway and on London's West End, generates substantial income from a single show. When the show becomes a staple, like *Rent* or *Fiddler on the Roof*, it can be performed repeatedly throughout the United States at legitimate theaters, dinner theaters, and in schools. The scripts and music are rented from one of several theatrical outfitters, such as Samuel French, and weekly royalties are paid, and then distributed to the show's authors. The fees are based on the seating capacity of the theater or auditorium, and the prices charged for tickets. A show that has a long track record of audience appreciation might be performed in literally hundreds of venues a year, bringing in further income for the show's creators.

When a soundtrack album is made, 40 percent of the royalties can go to the show's producer, and the remaining income is once again shared by the author of the book and the songwriters. According to the Brabec book mentioned in Chapter 7, this royalty varies from 1 to 4 percent. Of course, if the record doesn't recoup the cost of producing it, there are no royalties for anyone. This royalty does not include the mechanical income owing to the songwriters and publishers, which are distributed as they would be on any other record release. If songs from the soundtrack album are played on the radio, or performed on television, the songwriters get performance royalties just as they would for any airplay. If other revenue streams occur, such as merchandising rights for toys or games, or if the show is produced into a motion picture, the producer, obviously, also shares in the income from those revenue streams.

As the costs of mounting Broadway musicals have risen over ten million dollars, regional theaters such as the Denver Center for the Performing Arts, or the Mark Taper in Los Angeles, have become increasingly important in the development of new shows. Performances at these theaters also generate royalty percentages to the songwriters and author of the book.

When shows are written by authors who are not members of the Dramatists Guild, producers prefer to pay weekly salaries to the authors, rather than percentages. If the show is unsuccessful, this can actually work to the author's advantage. On the other hand, if the show is a great success, the authors will literally be sacrificing thousands or even hundreds of thousands of dollars in income.

For every show that becomes a success, there are dozens that never get produced, or that run for just a few weeks. When songs appear in a theatrical production, even if the show is not successful, it may result in other performances for the songs. Brian Gari's entertaining book, *We Bombed in New London: The Inside Story of the Broadway Musical, Late Night Comic*, describes this precise situation. In addition to performances in the defunct show, the songs were included in additional theatrical presentations, a record company issued a recording of the show, and Warner Brothers Music published a folio of songs from the show. All of this for a show that had only a handful of performances on Broadway!

Nevertheless, success brings virtually a lifetime annuity for publishers or creators of a hit show. A song from a successful Broadway musical can generate hundreds of thousands of dollars in ancillary revenues for the publisher and songwriters. Other possible successful outcomes from a Broadway show include hit singles and the use of the songs from the show in commercials. Since both the music and the words for Broadway shows tend to be more complex than the structure of the average pop song, and since there are thousands of aspiring actors and actresses who want to audition for other shows, sheet music is an important commodity in the Broadway community. One of the print publishers of the works will sub-license the print rights, in order to produce a folio for a hit show. The optimal return for the songwriter occurs when:

- the show is a long-running hit;

- road companies are formed for multiple performances;
- a hit single comes out of the soundtrack album, or from an artist not involved in the show;
- the soundtrack is a hit CD;
- the show is produced as a movie;
- a successful movie or DVD is produced, based on the show;
- some of the songs become standards;
- over the years, productions are mounted in schools and dinner theaters.

Although the above scenario is far from typical, it represents the best of all possible worlds. If every one of the possibilities outlined occurs, the show will generate millions of dollars in revenue for its creators, the producer, and the music publisher. If the show continues to be performed for many years, as is often the case with a major hit musical, revenue may be generated beyond the lifetime of the author, and for the remaining term of copyright protection.

The nature of print music

Print Rights relate to the exploitation of a work in printed form like piano vocal, folios, arrangements, or orchestrations which may be accompanied by audio or audiovisual components. In the early days of the music print business, the focus was on the music to individual songs. Over the years, the business has evolved into folios, collections of songs rather than individual ones. If you go to a store that specializes in sheet music you will see the following pop, rock, or country music selections:

- folios that contain the music to specific albums;
- folios that cover an entire career, e.g. *The John Denver Songbook*;
- mixed folio, e.g. *Songs of the Sixties*;
- sheet music to an individual song;
- large songbooks, e.g. *The Fireside Book of Folksongs*;
- Fake Books (discussed below).

Sometimes these are folios of songs that are performed, rather than written by the artist, for example *Songs of Celine Dionne*. Music print publishers also supervise the issue of songbooks and sheet music by their artists. The print publisher must have an agreement in place with the owner of the music copyright to authorize the print publication and sale of the song.

U.S. print royalties are paid by printers to the copyright owner that granted the print music license, usually the music publisher. The print licenses are usually non-exclusive and limited to three to five years in duration. For a single-song sheet music, publishers are usually paid 20 percent of the marked retail price (or about 80 cents @ $3.95 retail price). Folio royalties are paid at 10 to 12 percent of the marked retail price (or $1.50–$.80 @ $14.95 retail price). There is usually an extra 5 percent of marked retail price for personality folios, which require an additional license or consent for the right of publicity.

Foreign print music is collected by the foreign sub-publisher, who base their charge depending on whether they manufacture and sell the material. If the sub-publisher does manufacture the folio, they generally charge from 10 to 15 percent of the marked retail selling price. If they license out the print music, the sub-publisher retains the same percentage as all other income, generally 15 to 25 percent, and remits the balance to the publisher.

The royalty that goes from the print publisher to the publisher who owns the copyright is roughly 20 percent of the retail selling price of the book. The net songwriter's royalty share is negotiable, according to the overall terms of the publishing deal struck with the publisher. Some traditional book publishers compile large songbooks, licensing the print rights from print publishers. The book publisher will often seek to pay an outright fee for the song, for example, $250.00–$500.00, while the print publisher may seek a royalty, or a larger fee. Variables such as the stature and fame of the song are important considerations when negotiating a fee. Print publishers are not compelled by the copyright law to license their songs to others, nor do copyright owners have to license their songs to print publishers. Print royalties are usually paid on the basis of "net paid sales"—gross shipments, less returns, for which the publisher received payment.

The market for educational music

There is an entirely different market for print music that is used for educational purposes in schools, by music teachers, or people seeking to improve their musical skills. Hal Leonard and Alfred

Music are two companies active in this marketplace, as are Mel Bay and Neil Kjos. Today, Mel Bay is the primary publisher of guitar music in the world, with hundreds of publications running the gamut from classical to flamenco, rock and roll, jazz and folk guitar. The company now publishes music for numerous other instruments as well, and runs a record label. Guitar remains the cornerstone of their musical efforts.

Many of the instructional folios published by the companies listed above have started to include audio programs. At first, paper sound sheets were used, by Music Sales, Inc., in particular. As more and more musicians came along who did not read music, the sound sheets enabled them to hear the music printed in the books. The sound sheets were replaced by cassettes, and today, a good many instructional folios have CDs bound into the books. On the CDs, the author plays the printed selections, and often-times adds some spoken tips for the aspiring player. Some of the instructional books are now accompanied by DVDs, which enable the player not only to hear the music, but to see how the instructor holds the instrument, moves his hands, breathes, and so on.

Instructional materials: method books and solos

There are two basic types of instructional books. Method books are graded studies that are intended to teach the student in a cumulative fashion. Collections of solos are not necessarily put together in the same manner as method books, but are simply solos that the player feels will be beneficial for people to learn. In some cases, they are transcriptions of materials that appear on a CD, whose degree of difficulty may vary greatly from one piece to another. Some method books have been in print for years, and have been translated into many foreign languages. *The John Thompson Piano Method* has been in print for many years, and has sold literally millions of copies. It is published by Willis Music in Cincinnati, and distributed by Hal Leonard.

Many of the instructional books include new music composed by the author-teacher, or songs in the public domain. When copyrighted songs are used, they must be licensed from the copyright owner, and the fee must be negotiated. Often the authors of these books avoid using any copyrighted songs, because the royalties paid for the use of the copyrights are deducted from the royalties paid to the author of the book. In other cases, the author gets permission from the publisher to use the copyrighted tune without payment, because it is hoped that publication will help to promote a writer's career. Although the print business is not the bonanza it was in 1900, the consolidation of print companies, together with a relatively stable market for instructional materials, continues to grow this portion of the market.

Talented and committed singers or instrumentalists should consider the possibility of writing books for a print publisher like Mel Bay, Hal Leonard, or Alfred Music. This can provide a regular royalty stream to supplement emerging songwriting activities. To pitch a project to these companies, submit an outline of the project, a table of contents with estimated length of the book, a market analysis of where your project fits into the marketplace, and what niche it will satisfy that isn't currently being served by existing publications. Generally, these companies have relatively small staffs, and you should receive a quick response about whether they are interested in your project.

Fake Books

Fake Books are collections of songs which display simplified versions of a song's melody line, chords, and lyrics. A fairly basic musician can turn to a song in a Fake Book, and play the song right off the page, without any prior preparation. For many years, print publishers refused to issue Fake Books. There were several reasons behind this refusal. First of all, it was a nuisance to license, for example, one thousand songs in a single book. Second, the copyright owners had a limited degree of enthusiasm about licensing, for example, one out of a thousand songs, and receiving a royalty of one thousandth of the total royalty. If the Fake Book sold for $30.00, the entire royalty to the music publishers who owned 1,000 copyrights would be $6.00. One thousandth of $6.00 does not cover the cost of preparing the license (or even the postage).

There was, and still is, a great demand for Fake Books among musicians, because musicians playing a four-hour gig could use one or two Fake Books, and be able to perform the bulk of audience requests. The alternative was to bring several dozen songbooks to the job. Some of the Fake Books contained modern jazz tunes that had never been printed at all, so they were valuable tools for jazz musicians. Consequently, Fake Books were indeed published, albeit illegally. Every professional musician seemed to know someone who sold Fake Books. They were usually poorly printed, poorly bound books that sold for $50.00, or more. They also often contained musical errors.

Finally, in the early 1970s, a music print executive named Herman Steiger decided that it was time to legalize what was going on. He compiled the first legal Fake Book. Today, every print publisher has published these collections. There are jazz collections, country music, rock, and pop Fake Books, and they often sell for about $30.00. Known as a "pennies business," Steiger was apparently able to convince the publishing community that small royalties eventually add up to larger royalties.

School band and choral music

There is a large demand for band and choral music in schools, even though school music programs have experienced some serious budget cuts over the last ten years. Virtually every state has a music educators' organization with an annual meeting. The print publishers attend these meetings, and often give away CDs of their new band and/or choral arrangements. Since a large number of school music teachers attend these meetings, it is a good venue for promoting these products.

Print publishers also do mailings to junior and senior high-school band directors, sending samples of new arrangements, and often including CDs.

On a college level, there are two large annual national music conferences, the MENC (Music Educators National Conference) and the CMS (College Music Society). Print publishers exhibit at these events, and so do such book publishers as W. W. Norton and Oxford University Press, who publish everything from books about jazz or music theory to music history texts. Another organization, NAJE (the National Association of Jazz Educators), also has a national meeting where print publishers can display their jazz-oriented band music.

Most large cities have at least one store that specializes in choral music. There is also a good market for choral music in churches. Choral arrangements are sold for less than $2 per song, and the composer royalty rate is usually 10 percent of the retail selling price. In the church environment, the emphasis is not on hit songs, allowing for the exposure and sale of new music.

10 Foreign publishing revenue, rights, and deals

Copyright issues and intellectual property rights are, in fact, part of a global system. They operate within national jurisdictions, but copyright standards are part of an international system operating, in many cases, through international treaties.

Foreign Sub-Publishing Deals

Foreign Sub-Publishing entails the administration of rights and the exploitation of works in a foreign territory, via a license from the Original Publisher. There are two predominant strategies for managing music copyrights in foreign territories. One method is to grant the world-wide foreign rights, outside of the Original Territory, to a single publisher, in a "Rest-of-World" (RoW) deal. The other method, a Territory Deal, is to negotiate individual deals, territory-by-territory, whereby an Original Publisher is typically represented by different sub-publishers in each of the prominent foreign countries or territories throughout the world. There are advantages to each mode of operation. In an RoW deal, it is clearly convenient to have a single publisher represent a catalogue throughout the world. Obviously, a small U.S. publisher cannot afford the expense of having offices in various countries around the world. It is simply a convenience to sub-license these rights to one global publishing entity. There are also significant advantages to having all global royalties and registrations coordinated within a single coordinating publisher. The foreign sub-publisher will normally charge 10–20 percent of the gross collected income in their territory, and distribute the balance to the U.S. publisher. The commission charged by the sub-publisher is entirely negotiable. On the other hand, the advantages of separate, independent "territory" deals include: (1) more individualized creative attention to your catalogue; (2) more individualized administrative and financial attention to your catalogue; (3) greater flexibility in negotiating commissions and fees structures; and (4) greater flexibility in negotiating the substantive terms and conditions of the Sub-Publishing Agreement. In either deal, the original publisher reserves all rights in the music and all copyright for all areas outside of the defined foreign territory.

Many of the Foreign Sub-Publishing and Representation Deals are made at MIDEM, the annual international music business conference in Cannes, France. Held each year in January, MIDEM offers comprehensive music business conference programs, with nearly 10,000 music and technology professionals from over ninety different countries in attendance. Major music and media companies, as well as independent writers and publishers, meet with the recording, publishing, live, digital, mobile, and branding sectors to negotiate deals, network, learn the latest updates impacting international publishing rights, and check out new talent. Nearly all of the world's independent sub-publishers attend MIDEM, in an effort to introduce themselves, and structure administration and Representation Deals for their catalogues throughout the world.

Functions of sub-publishers

Agreements between Original Publishers and foreign sub-publishers can be on a Collection Deal basis, or a "Representation" basis. Original Territory music publishers select catalogue representatives in foreign territories—sub-publishers—who take on the traditional publisher functions, on behalf of the Original Publisher and its catalogue, within a defined country or territory. In a Collection Deal, the primary job of the local publisher in the foreign territory is to collect income that is generated and earned by the catalogue in that territory. In a Representation Deal, the primary job of the local sub-publisher is to obtain new uses of the Original Publisher's songs in the local territory, including (1) pitching songs for local cover recordings, (2) obtaining and coordinating translations of lyrics into the local foreign language, and (3) pitching songs for local placements in film, television, commercials, or print music uses.

Exploitation

In a Representation Deal (or "Exploitation Deal"), the sub-publisher is called upon to obtain "local covers" and placements of a writer's works in its local territory. The sub-publisher in these types of deals will generally earn a higher percentage of income than in a Collection Deal, since it is obvious that the sub-publisher generates additional income by actually procuring recordings for songs, in addition to the collection of royalties on the Original Publisher/artist's own recordings when they are released in the foreign territory. There are two distinct opportunities to be achieved in foreign Representation Deals: (1) a U.S. publisher will seek to have its copyrights represented in foreign territories in an effort to obtain new recordings of existing songs that were produced in the United States. Depending upon the musical style involved, the publisher may also want to have the original lyrics translated into other languages, for maximum exposure and commercial success in local markets. Additionally, (2) some of the copyrights that the foreign publisher owns or controls may be songs that can be exploited in the United States, providing an opportunity for the U.S. publisher to represent a broader catalogue of songs. Representation commissions vary, according to many factors, but can range from 20 to 50 percent of income earned by procuring a local cover. If a foreign language translation of a song is obtained, the local sub-publisher will seek an income participation or copyright share of that particular version of the song, and the translator will also seek a percentage of the songwriter's income.

A songwriter who is also a recording artist should view exploitation of her songs in foreign territories not only as a source of immediate income, but as an opportunity to create exposure, interest, and local consumer demand for the artist-writer to tour in that country, creating a new market in which to sell records.

A variety of possible foreign opportunities for songs are available, including:

- An American recording artist who is fluent in several languages, records a song in French and Spanish. The song becomes a hit in the United States in the English version, and the French and Spanish versions become major sellers in Latin America and Europe.

- A song that never achieved success in the United States captures the attention of a foreign audience.
- A song is performed at a European songwriters' festival, resulting in successful European recordings, in different languages.
- An American commercial is used on Japanese television, with the lyric translated into Japanese.
- A song that hasn't been heard in the United States in years becomes a pop hit in a foreign territory, generating significant new radio performances and income.
- A little-known American song is used as the theme for a foreign TV show.

Administration

For a negotiated percentage of the gross income collected in the applicable foreign territory, the foreign publisher in a Collection Deal will collect music royalties and license fees generated within a defined territory, as agreed to in the Sub-Publishing Agreement. Collecting royalties in foreign territories presents unique challenges, justifying the use of local publishers who understand the language and who have relationships with the local royalty collection agencies. Major artists would likely have Collection Deals, since most of their income is derived from the sale of their own records. The principal functions of a foreign sub-publisher in a Collection Deal include: (1) registration of the songs with the performance and mechanical royalty societies in the local territory; (2) coordinating and supervising translations and uses of the original works; and (3) collection of royalties generated in the local territory. It is not uncommon for U.S. song titles, especially when used in foreign television shows, to be translated into the foreign language. Finding the uses, re-translating the titles, and accounting for the royalties that have been earned, can be daunting, technical tasks. The collection fee (administration fee) charged by the foreign sub-publisher is usually between 10 and 15 percent of gross royalties collected in the local territory. The sub-publisher is responsible for registering the work with the performing rights societies in the territory, insuring that the publisher's performance and broadcast royalties are properly and accurately credited and distributed to the Original Publisher. If a publisher does not have a designated foreign sub-publisher collecting its share in each country, the foreign Performing Rights Organization (PRO) will forward the royalties to the publisher's U.S. PRO. The foreign Performing Rights Society in each territory (PRS in England, or SOCAN in Canada, for example), collects and forwards royalties for U.S. writers' works performed in their country to the writer's U.S. PRO for distribution to the writer in the United States. All such income is reported on U.S. royalty statements as "foreign income." As is the case with domestic performance rights distributions in the United States, foreign receipts are distributed by the U.S. performing rights organizations separately to their writer and publisher members. The U.S. PROs similarly collect performance income for foreign society writers and publishers whose works are performed in the United States. The monies collected are forwarded to the foreign society of which the writer or publisher is a member.

Foreign collections

The calculations of royalty payments received in the Original Territory from foreign sub-publishers are dependent on whether the royalty payments are calculated on an "at-source" or "receipts" basis. In an "at-source" deal, the royalties flowing to the Original Publisher are based on the income in the country where earned (e.g. France), which is considered the "source." There are no additional deductions, fees or offsets charged against the source royalties, other than the authorized administration fee.

In a "receipts" deal, the royalties flowing to the Original Publisher can reflect expenses and deductions that may be charged against the gross royalties collected. The receipts, therefore, are "net" royalties, after accounting for the administration fee, as well as expenses and fees on earnings in the country where received (e.g. United States). "At-source" deals, therefore, generally tend to maximize income for songwriters.

Foreign mechanical royalties

In the United Sates, mechanical royalties are paid on a song-by-song basis, at the statutory rate currently in effect, for sales of records embodying a composition. Unlike the United States, foreign mechanical societies grant mechanical licenses for the entire record based on a percentage of the wholesale or retail price, regardless of the number of songs. BIEM, a mechanical collection society, represents all of Europe, and establishes a royalty rate which is based on the "Published Price to Dealers" (PPD). PPDs are typically priced between the wholesale and retail selling price of the product. The current BIEM-established royalty rate is 6.5 percent of the PPD price. This represents the total royalty payable by the record company for all of the compositions contained on that record. The separate compositions are then accounted for on a time/duration basis, and the 6.5 percent royalty is allocated, in pro rata shares, to each of the songs on the CD. Comparison of the European method with the United States method usually results in a higher royalty being paid in Europe on a per-record basis.

11 New media, technology, and copyright

Technology overview

As we write this book, the first decade of the twenty-first century is coming to a close. Technology writers seem to fall into two camps. There are the enthusiasts, who see the Internet and the digital revolution as the panacea that will bring the world together, and there are the nay-sayers who fear the unknown, and who are unable to adapt to new technologies. At the close of the twentieth century, we saw the introduction of the MP3 format, and the advent of ground-breaking file sharing programs, such as Napster, Kazaa, and Grokster.

As technological advances have introduced new products and techniques to the world of audio recording, musicians have been increasingly displaced by the technology. Music producers began to replace musicians with digital recording equipment, music software programs, electronic scores, synthesizers, and samplers. Currently, some touring Broadway shows are using an electronic synthesizer called the Virtual Orchestra, and Broadway orchestras are increasingly relying on electronic instruments and drum machines. Various dance companies, as well, are using one or another version of taped music or the Virtual Orchestra in their performances.

Karaoke and club disc jockeys have also diminished employment opportunities for live musicians. In Portland, Oregon, disc jockeys are beginning to apply for membership in the musician's union, leaving the union membership in the position of determining the question of whether a DJ is a musician.

Recording technology

The recording studio business has also experienced radical changes as a result of technological innovation. Many projects are now recorded in a digital suite of software programs, such as Pro Tools, rather than with analog tape. This is digital, computer-based recording, and can readily be done in a home studio with consumer computer equipment. The negative impact on commercial studios has been significant, as many sophisticated recording projects can now be completed in home studios, and without any support from third-party recording budgets. Commercial studios are often used solely for the final mixing and/or mastering, thereby cutting down their share of the money budgeted for recording. With the growing sophistication and affordability of audio software programs and digital instrumentation, fewer recording sessions require large orchestras, thereby greatly reducing the need for studios to have large recording rooms, or employ numerous musicians. A single "producer" can now assume the roles of composer, musician(s), engineer, and producer of the project.

New media and the Internet

Outside of the recording studio, itself, a musician's greatest technological tool may now be the Internet. Whether used for market research, education, promotion, marketing, advertising, i-session global recordings, or sales, the Internet provides access and opportunity to every musician and band . . . no matter where you live. As has been well documented, the Internet also poses serious threats for traditional copyright ownership, and the traditional record label model. The once-daunting barrier of obtaining major label distribution for independent artists is eroding, as the mechanics of Internet sales become increasingly easy, affordable, and understandable. Placing a CD or an individual song for sale on any of the nearly fifty digital store websites, including CDbaby.com, Amazon.com, or iTunes.com, establishes global presence for your music. "Digital Aggregators" (Ioda, The Orchard, Big Fish Media), much like their physical CD counterparts, are the new distributors of downloadable CDs, and greatly facilitate the process of placing CDs for sale at Internet retail sites throughout the world. It is not uncommon for unsigned, independent artists to sell several thousand CDs from their own website and Internet retailers. Selling even a few thousand CDs, when you keep nearly $8 to $10 per CD, can generate significant income.

In addition to providing a worldwide "retail store" for selling CDs, the Internet also allows for a very affordable means of staying in contact with an artist's fan base. Newsletters, schedules of upcoming concert tours, and band merchandise are now all within easy access of every fan . . . and soon-to-become fans. Gone are the days when radio airplay is the only means of getting music heard . . . or of generating any news or excitement about an act. Internet promotion, or "viral" word-of-mouth, is rapidly becoming a mainstream, inexpensive way to advertise and market an artist.

Other significant technological advances are also changing the way that music can be marketed and promoted. Advances in cell phone technology and wireless platforms can now link iPods, iPhones, home computers, stereos, and car sound systems into a seamless, commercial-free music zone. The services will allow new phones to function as music hubs, enabling the download of songs, television episodes, and radio programming from an Internet-connected device, and opening the door for ever-widening exposure (and sales) of songs and music videos.

Blogs, the virtually free means to publish and post articles, commentary, music, and videos through online "web-logs," and podcasting, the emerging technology that allows individuals to create and store their own radio broadcasts and deliver them over the Web, are both significant factors in allowing artists to promote their music, from their home, at very low cost. As these technological advances gain mainstream acceptance, the savvy musician can take advantage of one or more of these tools in her attempt to gain a wider audience. The notion that an artist can make a living in a local hometown music market is rapidly becoming a realistic, practical, and preferred path to commercial success.

Copyright on the Internet

Notwithstanding the incredible opportunities provided by the Internet, the threat of copyright piracy—the use of someone else's creative work without permission or compensation—has also grown with the global embrace of the Web. The Internet has given every person on earth with a computer and access to a modem the ability to engage in the unauthorized, mass distribution of any type of creative work. Copyright protections, therefore, may become even more important in the digital world than in the physical one. The U.S. Copyright Act itself explicitly recognizes that facts and ideas are not protectable, and may be distributed freely by and among members of the public. It is the *expression* of those facts and ideas that is protectable, so as to encourage creativity. Music and other works that entertain us constitute expression and are subject to copyright protection as a property right. Just as the law protects us against someone driving away with our car without permission, it also enables a songwriter or a music copyright owner to prevent someone from taking his work without permission and selling it or distributing it to vast numbers of people on the Internet. For creators, this is not only a matter of fairness, but of economic survival.

Technology and copyright

As technology advanced, and the accessibility to music over the Internet (both legal and illegal) became increasingly more available, a number of musicians and legal scholars began to question many of the basic tenets that have governed the Copyright Act and the concept of intellectual property rights.

One of the first controversies that emerged involved taking an existing work and transforming it into a different, but related, artistic creation. Walt Disney Studios famously took fairy tales and bits of folklore and changed them into "new," and, of course, copyrighted works. In the world of rock and roll, the band *Negativland* and a British band called *The Jams* were fond of the use of collage. Collage is a technique where the artist takes a pre-existing work, and uses snippets of it along with something new and entirely different. As recording technology became cheap, digital, and widely available, accomplishing such alchemy became a simple matter. Meanwhile in the world of hip hop music, producers and artists began to take existing recorded sounds and to superimpose them on new works, creating "mash-ups." For example, they would take a scream by James Brown and interpolate it into a new piece of music.

The use of previously recorded sounds became known as sampling, and it began to be heavily employed in the 1980s. Not surprisingly, the copyright owners screamed "foul," and threatened lawsuits. The resolution of sampling is not so much based on court-cases, but more on a kind of gentleman's agreement between record companies, brokered by lawyers.

The same two rights that are involved with samples are involved with the ownership of all recordings: the ownership of the Master Recording of the performance, and the ownership of the underlying musical Composition. The record producer and/or the record label that produces the new work must negotiate for the use of the existing rights. Since the authors of the Copyright Act never anticipated such a "sampling" right, there were no established royalty rates set. It was a matter of negotiation between the various parties involved. Some of the elements that govern the license fee include how recognizable the sampled sound is, whether the original copyright is valuable, and the length of the sample being used.

As technology continued to advance, some of the users of samples began to disguise the borrowed items. Musical pitch and tone could be affected by speeding up or slowing down the tape, or sometimes the sample was overlaid with other sounds so that only the person who was doing the sampling would know what was being sampled. Alternative rock artists, notably Moby and Beck, also jumped on the sampling wagon, and sampled everything from field recordings of chain gang singers to famous hit records. Record companies reacted with panic, and began to require producers to keep track of every single sample that they had used, no matter how obscure.

Sometimes the lawsuits that resulted from the use of sampling crossed over into the bizarre. There is a very famous avant garde piece of classical music entitled *4'33"*, credited to John Cage. We say credited, because the piece consists entirely of silence. When the piece is "performed," so to speak, the silence evaporates because the audience coughs, moves back and forth in its seats, mutters, fidgets, and so forth. An artist named Mike Bot "sampled" one minute of this piece and was sued by Cage's publisher for infringement of copyright. (One can imagine all sorts of humorous conceivable lawsuits based on the same notion. For example, should the publisher have sued religious orders where the participants undertake the vow of silence? And should these people have defended the suit by claiming that they had pre-existing ownership in this somewhat-mythical copyright?)

File sharing

A record company has many sources of revenue, including legal digital distribution, Master licensing to film, television, and commercials, and in many cases, the ownership of music publishing rights. The artist can generate revenues through performances and the sale of merchandise. The songwriter whose songs are illegally downloaded receives nothing in return, unless you consider that any resulting airplay and performance rights royalties may serve as adequate compensation for the theft of his writer's mechanical royalties.

Digital works are easily and exactly copied via file sharing, and impact all contributors and owners of copyrighted material. The recording and motion picture industries maintain that unauthorized file sharing, along with the production and sale of pirated hard copies of CDs and DVDs, have resulted in billions of dollars of lost sales, and it has been well documented that sales of CDs have been declining for the last five years. Various experts lay the blame in different places. Some fault MP3 technology and Napster and their successors for creating an environment where many young people (and some older ones) feel that they no longer need to pay for music, and can simply rip whatever tunes they want from the Internet. Attempts to prevent this have been largely unsuccessful, though some organizations such as the Recording Industry Association of America (RIAA) and the Motion Picture Association of America (MPAA) have begun to sue individual violators that they can identify, and to force file sharing networks to either shut down or pay damages, or both. There have been many newspaper and magazine articles that detail the suits against grandmothers, parents, and college students over their ripping hundreds of songs off the Net. The National Music Publishers Association (NMPA) has taken action to remove lyrics and guitar instructional materials from the Internet in the same way that the RIAA has sued or threatened file sharers who rip recordings. Prior to their actions, a fair amount of lyrics and instructional materials were available on the Net. The NMPA has forced this material off the Internet because the works are copyrighted, and no payment was offered to the copyright owners. Possibly, if the RIAA spent more energy explaining the disastrous financial effects of file sharing on songwriters, the young file sharers would be a bit more sympathetic.

Ambiguity in the interpretation of copyright law, coupled with rapid and continual advances in digital technologies, have been major factors contributing to the lack of successful enforcement by the intellectual property owners. In looking to the future, rights owners rely on the fact that most people still obtain music, and especially movies, through authorized channels of distribution, a situation they hope to maintain by increasing the availability of authorized online services (such as Apple's iTunes).

Evolving entertainment industry models

Global sales of music CDs and DVDs dipped for the sixth consecutive year in 2005, the most recent year of complete data. Worldwide sales, including physical and digital formats, fell to about $21 billion in wholesale revenue in 2005. On a retail basis, the industry generated about $33 billion in sales in 2005, a decline of nearly 3 percent, according to the annual report released by the trade group, the International Federation of the Phonographic Industry (IFPI). In the United States, wholesale revenues generated by sales of physical CDs and DVDs in 2005 was about $7 billion, a decline of 9 percent; while overall shipments of music products, including digital downloads, declined only 3.9 percent, according to the RIAA.

Sales of digital music are rising sharply, but they do not compensate for the decline of CDs, which have been the recording industry mainstay for two decades. The number of single songs downloaded online or to mobile phones, as tracks, ringtones, and ringbacks, rose more than 190 percent, to nearly 450 million units in 2005, representing a twenty-fold increase over 2004. Revenue from digital sales in 2006 nearly tripled, to $1.1 billion from $400 million in 2005, according to IFPI. Clearly, digital music sales are having a significant, positive impact on traditional music industry business models.

Other reasons for the decline in record sales are given as the increasing popularity of video games, the availability of DVDs at virtually the same price as CDs, the availability of reasonably priced used CDs, and the consumers' feeling that CDs are overpriced. In fact the price structure of CDs is confusing. Most consumers are aware of the fact that the cost of manufacturing CDs has greatly diminished. Even an independent artist can buy a thousand copies of a CD from a manufacturer for about a dollar a CD. What is confusing to the consumer is that prices have crept up to almost $20.00 per unit. At the same time, record companies have introduced their "midlevel" product which retails at about half that price. The consumer infers that clearly the retail price of new products has been inflated. When the consumer sees the specials at the discount stores, further confusion is created. The typical consumer doesn't understand the concept of a loss leader, they are confused that a $19.00 item can be sold for $9.95, while catalogue products may be selling, even at discount, for $15.00 or $16.00.

Another measure of the effects of record discounters' presence, together with the impact of illegal downloads, is that the number of independent record retailers declined from seven thousand outlets to two thousand outlets, in the period from 1991 to 2006. These figures come from the "Changes Afoot" article, written by Todd Martens in the March 31, 2007 issue of music trade paper *Billboard*.

Although the major labels are having difficulty surviving in today's world of lower sales, increased illegal file sharing, fewer record stores, and the narrow-casting mentality of radio stations, a new set of entrepreneurs is entering the marketplace. These are companies that are not centered on the entertainment business, but are using music, media, and entertainment as a means of attracting customers to their core businesses.

The Hallmark greeting card company has issued several successful CDs, including a recent full-length CD of classic jazz tracks. Their James Taylor CD was actually more successful than his most recent major label efforts. For years, Nordstrom's, an up-scale northwestern department store, has featured live piano music in their stores, and now they too have started a record label. When Toyota wanted to attract younger customers to their Scion model, they started a record label, signing two acts. Toyota also established a business model of co-owning the recordings with the artists.

Starbucks has been selling compilation recordings for several years, licensing the music from existing labels. In a new joint venture, Concord Music Group, Starbucks' partner in its Hear Music label, has released Paul McCartney's latest record, with a plan to use Starbucks' 13,500 retail outlets to sell the album. Hear Music's multi-pronged marketing strategy includes releas-ing McCartney's music via online download sites, and in Hear

Music coffee houses, where fans can burn tracks onto CDs. This innovative sales platform reaches 44 million customers per week through Starbucks stores.

Another recent development centers on the success that accompanied the transformation of background television music tracks to CDs. Warner Brothers Records has made a deal with Alex Patsavas, the music supervisor behind the successful *O.C.* and *Grey's Anatomy* soundtrack albums. She will have her own label imprint, and she will sign acts and create an A&R staff. Another label, Putamayo, started out as a small subsidiary of an import clothing business, but became so successful that the president of the company left the clothing business and now runs the record label. Putamayo CDs are sold in record stores, but can also be found in clothing stores, New Age outlets, and in supermarkets that specialize in natural foods. Another label, Sounds True, specializes in world music and music utilized for spiritual and healing purposes. Their CDs tend to be found in outlets similar to where Putamayo places its music.

Ironically, just as major labels seem to be presiding over a crumbling superstructure, new labels are being born that are focused on specific aspects of music or are tied in to existing business structures that have built-in distribution capability. Songwriters and publishers may well find interesting new outlets for songs by exploiting these opportunities. In a rapidly evolving marketplace, even established artists are experimenting with new business and revenue models.

REALWORLD: Radiohead: "pay what you want"

Radiohead, one of the world's most acclaimed rock bands, has made its recent album, *In Rainbows* (October, 2007) available on its website as a digital download, with no set price. The British band has elected to sidestep the conventional music industry distribution, sales, and royalty protocols with its self-released new album, posting a message on its website that reads: "It's up to you." The band became a free agent following its 2003 release of *Hail to the Thief* on EMI Records. Acknowledging that the "pay what you want" pricing policy is an experiment, Radiohead has placed itself at the crossroads of traditional industry business models, and the evolving new marketplace. As the old record models are facing increasing consumer pressures, Radiohead is attempting to redefine the value of music, the manner in which artists relate to their fans, and the underlying economic and financial rewards that derive from intellectual property and copyright ownership. "We've seen the crumbling of bigger labels, but there haven't been any big 'Aha!' moments . . . that risky departure," claims *Wired* magazine editor Nancy Miller. "It's an interesting move, a terrific example of an artist exerting a terrific amount of control; it's definitely going to be successful."

The ironic prosperity of the music publishing business

Record stores are struggling financially, major labels' sales are significantly reduced, and most independent labels aren't doing all that well. Music publishers, however, are faring surprisingly well in this environment. Here are some of the reasons:

- there is an increasing number of emerging film and television opportunities;
- the growth of legal digital downloads;
- the expansion of ringtones and ringbacks;
- audio and video Internet streaming, and other mobile and wireless platforms;
- increased use of existing songs for commercials and advertising campaigns;
- expanding satellite and Internet radio uses;
- increasing value of performance rights;
- the growth of video game licenses;
- traditional promotional expenses have decreased;
- a small but steady increase in the print music business.

At a music business seminar in Los Angeles in March, 2007, a music V.P. of Fox Sports Network estimated that he uses over a million and a half pieces of music in a single year! Of course, many of these cues are for five or ten seconds, but all of them must be properly licensed from their own music library, or from third-party music libraries, or from individual publishers and the record companies. This is just one indication of the explosion of the use of music in contemporary music programming and production. Ringtones and ringbacks are an additional unexpected recent royalty bonanza for songwriters and publishers. Ringtones can generate a royalty of approximately ten to twelve cents for each download, although some are licensed on a percentage of the charge from the phone company. Although the use of ringtones is relatively new and rapidly growing in the United States, they have been widely used and have been a significant royalty revenue source from Europe and Asia, for several years.

Telecommunication and record companies are now also heavily promoting the notion of full-song downloads via cell phones, and the delivery of music over cell phones by selling subscriptions. Fan club advertising is beginning to appear on text messages, and other promotional messages will inevitably appear on camera phones. The latter are only just now becoming available to the American consumer. In the near future, concert tickets will also be available via mobile phones. As the sound quality of cell phones improves, it will create an ever-expanding market for musical products. New media royalties generated from audio and visual streaming sites, download sites, cell phone ringtones and ringbacks, and ancillary wireless devices have become a significant new source of income for writers and publishers.

Although they are a rapidly growing source of income, Internet radio license fees are currently under negotiation. The challenge in determining a fair Internet license fee is that the largest providers, such as Yahoo, can afford to pay far more than a community radio station in a small town. Somehow, a viable compromise must be made between the rates paid by large and small providers. It is likely that a compromise could be negotiated similar to that of the existing PRO licenses with radio stations, which are based on the gross advertising revenues the broadcaster. BMI and ASCAP are currently negotiating with satellite radio to determine exactly what royalties will be paid for satellite transmissions. Since XM and Sirius, the two existing companies, are currently attempting to merge, the disposition of these rights may take a while to resolve.

In addition to new media income, the increased use of songs in commercials and branded advertising campaigns is yet another significant and rapidly growing income source for publishers. In previous years, advertising music consisted primarily of newly created production material composed under work-for-hire agreements, and often published by the advertising agency.

Representing a major source of income for writers and publishers, ASCAP and BMI license collections have increased nearly every year in the last decade. Currently, they each collect approximately $700 million a year, with ASCAP reporting $785 million of revenue in 2006, representing a 5 percent growth over the previous year. This reflects the increasing value of performance rights in new media, cable television, and expanding ancillary opportunities. It also represents a marked contrast with the downward spiral of sales of recorded music. Publishers are also enjoying increased royalties from the use of music in video games, background music services (such as Muzak and AEI), and specialty store branded compilations.

Digital music uses and the singer-songwriter

Even if we ignore the problems of illegal downloading, digital uses of music pose some problems for both the artist and the songwriter. Most recordings in today's market utilize a high degree of technology, and the artist, record producer, and engineer spend many hours in their attempts to get the best possible sound. The truth is that many people will be listening to these recordings via MP3s on a computer, or on iPods, with small speakers or ear buds.

Another problem is just as serious. The singer-songwriter or recording artist often conceives of an album as being the realization of a concept. In other words the songs are inter-related, and they are placed in a particular order on the album for very specific and artistic reasons. When a consumer rips one song from an album like the Beatles' Sergeant Pepper, they are basically editing the singer-songwriter's work, and hearing it in a context in which it may not have been intended to be heard. This has to be irritating to the singer-songwriter.

Challenges to Copyright Law

Several popular music websites consist largely of a network of users who—without authorization—make and distribute to one another derivative works and full-length copies of other people's copyrighted musical compositions. These unauthorized copies take the form of both sheet music and audio versions, and are impacting songwriters, publishers, recording artists, and record labels. These distributions are in clear violation of the exclusive rights granted to creators and copyright owners under the U.S. Copyright Act and other national laws to make, arrange, and distribute works.

Thousands of Internet users derive substantial economic benefits by getting reams of sheet music or hours of audio for free, and in the process, displacing millions of dollars in sales and royalties which would have gone to support the creators and copyright owners of the works utilized. Such infringing websites are essentially part of a massive barter network in which goods that do not belong to the users are traded back and forth to the enormous detriment of the true owners. Recognizing the danger posed by infringing websites, and even "barter sites," Congress recently enacted legislation to criminalize the activities of Internet pirates who upload protected works for the purpose of making them available to a mass audience without authorization, irrespective of whether such infringement is carried out for personal financial gain. Operators of infringing music sites should be aware that their activities could fall within the scope of this criminal law, known as the No Electronic Theft Act.

Particularly among younger buyers, when someone rips a recording without payment, the offender may not see it as stealing from the artist. Further along the path of rationalization is the notion that superstar acts don't need the money anyway. In an attempt to justify their activities, many unauthorized music users have rationalized their actions as hurting only those stars "who are already rich." Economically successful music creators and companies are not the principal victims of cyber-theft, however. The music community consists mainly of thousands of small, struggling publishers and little-known songwriters, and it is their ability to survive that is most strongly and adversely affected by copyright infringement, whether online or otherwise.

Some argue that such theft actually serves the interests of its victims. Several legal scholars, notably Stanford University professor and lawyer Lawrence Lessig, and the Electronic Frontier Foundation (EFF), take the position that, in an information economy, the true scarce commodity is human attention. They contend that songwriters and musicians should "give away their songs and products—to purchase attention." In their view, attracting that attention will be the necessary precondition of generating sales, and the real source of wealth.

"You sell more records and get more exposure as a result of our activities," is a familiar claim. Indeed, a growing number of artists, themselves, support file sharing of their own works, arguing that it expands their audience to include people who would not otherwise be able or willing to legally purchase their material.

REALWORLD: **Progressive digital strategies**

The Crimea, a British rock act, has taken a progressive approach to building a fan base. The band—currently out of contract with their former label—has made its new, self-financed, album, *Secrets of the Witching Hour*, available to download—for free—from their official website (a CD version of the record will be offered for sale on a mail-order basis). The band members look for the free offering to generate exposure and, in turn, boost revenue streams from live performances and merchandise sales. "It's a one-off for us," their manager says. "The band knew they couldn't compete in the traditional way, so why not give it away, and try to gain more exposure that way. If we can get the fan base up significantly, maybe someone would be interested in doing a partnership with the band."

Broadcasters frequently claim that they should get free use of music because the exposure they provide helps to sell records. Users ranging from film and television producers to restaurant and club owners have made similar assertions. Record manufacturers have argued for free use, claiming that without the widespread availability of recordings, songs would never get airplay. Producers of Fake Books (sheet music pirates) have made all of the above claims. With all of these "friends" of the music community helping to boost the popularity of songs through their unauthorized uses, creators would likely starve without proper protection and enforcement through the copyright laws. Many infringing website administrators argue that they are different because no one "profits" from their allegedly "non-commercial" uses. However, as noted above, thousands of users do derive substantial economic benefits by getting reams of sheet music or hours of audio for free. This is not an activity that courts are likely to determine constitutes Fair Use.

Many of Professor Lessig's challenges have raised concerns about the application and interpretation of the U.S. copyright laws, as well as the duration of copyright protections accorded to original works. Lessig and his peers argue that the current term of copyright protection—life of the composer plus seventy years—is actually an impediment to the creation of new artistic works. They cite patents, which are only valid for fourteen years, at which time they go into the public domain. Lessig's contention is that creativity may be stifled when an income stream is protected for lengthy periods. Another of Lessig's challenges revolves around the amount of effort that a copyright owner invests—or fails to invest—in promoting a specific work. If a copyrighted work goes un-promoted by an original owner, but subsequent success comes to the work through the efforts of persons other than the original owner, Lessig questions why the original "passive" copyright owner should participate in any of the revenues. It is rare, but not impossible, for publishers to become inactive, distracted, or incompetent. Lessig makes the argument that ownership of copyright assets should be an active, limited, hands-on privilege, and that intellectual property should enter the public domain with much fewer restrictions.

In his book, *Free Culture: The Nature and Future of Creativity*, Lessig makes another specific proposal concerning the duration of copyright, whereby a publisher could obtain seventy-five years of copyright protection, but would be required to renew the copyright every five years, or lose the protection of copyright. Lessig points out that 94 percent of the films, books, and music created and published between 1923 and 1946 are no longer commercially available, and should, therefore result in a "forfeiture," of sorts, of the copyright. Lessig's position, that a copyright owner would lose her copyright to the public domain if it were not properly maintained and preserved, not only ignores precedential copyright law, but it also ignores the rights of the underlying songwriter or creator of the original work. Why should a writer lose the protection of his rights because the publisher has failed to properly re-register a song? If Lessig's proposal were followed, it may be more reasonable to suggest that, if a publisher fails in its responsibilities to re-register a work, then the song would revert to the property of its author, as opposed to going into the public domain.

In 1999, Lessig took a case to the U.S. Supreme Court in an attempt to invalidate the 1998 Sonny Bono copyright extension law, on the grounds that the extended protection (life of the last surviving author, plus seventy years) violated the limited terms of protection specified in the U.S. Constitution and provisions of the First Amendment. Although generally considered to be aggressive interpretations of current copyright law, Lessig's views continue to raise issues that generate both controversy and contemplation in the copyright community. Notwithstanding his substantial credentials, Lessig's proposals have only gained the serious attention of a relatively small number of scholars and practitioners.

Copyright in the twenty-first century

Are there any solutions to the problem of illegal file sharing? Ultimately, the only solutions to the problem may be education and innovation. The young file-sharer needs to understand that if content providers cannot be compensated, then creators may turn to other professions. In addition to pursuing well-publicized law suits, record companies have aggressively attempted to develop protection systems that prevent the copying of recordings. To date, these efforts have fallen victim to an ever-present number of computer hackers who spend their time developing systems to defeat the protective codes.

An amusing sidelight to the whole picture is that the record companies all employ a company called Big Champagne. Big Champagne monitors what songs are being ripped, report that information (for a fee) to the record companies, and the companies then intensively promote the most popular ripped songs. Certain artists and record companies have also made downloads of certain songs for free, using this as a promotional tool to sell albums and promote concerts. Another tool that record companies have utilized is to give away DVDs, posters, or additional short CDs with the sale of new CDs. Since these perks can't be accessed on the Internet, the consumer is thus essentially being creatively guided to buy materials that they might have ripped off without the additional incentives.

As the Performing Rights Organizations have demonstrated through their very successful use of the blanket license, one of the key solutions to the problem of keeping music websites legal and available to enthusiasts is to devise and implement pragmatic licensing situations. Seeking permission to use music need not be difficult, burdensome, or costly. The PROs and the National Music Publishers Association (NMPA) are actively designing licensing protocols and methods to facilitate licensing of copyrighted works. The currently infringing sites can eventually develop into sites which serve the interests of all parties— including those who need to earn a living from their creative works now and those who hope to do so in the future—but only with the cooperation of those sites' users.

12 Legal issues and artist representation

This chapter provides an overview of some of the basic legal and copyright issues that are routinely found in agreements and negotiations surrounding copyright ownership, royalty distribution, and songwriter/artist representation. The authors strongly encourage the readers to seek the advice of an entertainment attorney when entering into any written agreement.

Limits and exceptions to copyright

Notwithstanding the breadth of U.S. copyright statutes, all copyrights, by law, eventually expire and the owner (or his heirs), therefore, would no longer retain exclusive rights to his works. And as a result of legal actions and revisions to the Copyright Act, there are also several statutory and legal limitations and exceptions to copyright law.

Public Domain

All compositions which are no longer protected under copyright law are said to be in the Public Domain (PD). If it can be verified that the duration of copyright protection in a musical work has expired—that the composition is in the Public Domain—you can (1) perform the work royalty-free, (2) make, publish, and copyright an arrangement, or derivative work, and (3) use or record the arrangement or derivative work—without seeking permission or a license from the original owner. PD songs, therefore, may be used for profit-making activities, without paying any royalties. Sound recordings, however, are protected separately from musical compositions, and they, too, enjoy copyright protections for a specified term of years. If you seek to use a sound recording—even a recording of a Public Domain song—you have the option of making a new recording of the song, yourself, or licensing a Master Recording from the Master owner.

Derivative works

When a musical work is first written down in a tangible form, the "original work" is created. Any subsequent change made to the original creates a new work, referred to as a "derivative work." The author of a work has exclusive rights not only to her original work, but also exclusive rights to make derivative works from the original. Once copyright protection has expired, however, and a work has fallen into the Public Domain, anyone is free to create and copyright a new derivative work based on the original. In this regard, a composition may have numerous derivative works protected by copyright, even if the original is the Public Domain.

Arrangements of Public Domain works

Although a music arranger does not typically participate in copyright ownership or in the songwriter or publisher royalties, the *arrangement of a PD song* can be protected by copyright. If you create a new version or derivative version of a Public Domain song, you can obtain a copyright in that specific, unique arrangement, and no one can use that arrangement without your permission. However, the underlying song remains in the Public Domain, and anyone else can also make and copyright her own version of the same PD song. A chord progression does not constitute an arrangement, and a chord progression alone cannot be protected by copyright. But the chord progression, harmonies, accompanying rhythm, and musical fill phrases, together, are a creative work which define the style and feel of a song. Even though a song may be in the Public Domain, there are frequently numerous copyrighted arrangements of any given PD work.

Fair Use

Copyright does not prohibit all copying or replication. Copyright law is written to encourage the growth of knowledge, while at the same time protecting those who further the growth of knowledge.

"Fair Use" is the concept within the copyright law which weighs the balance between use and protection. In the United States, the Fair Use doctrine, codified by the Copyright Act of 1976 as 17 U.S.C. Section 107, permits some copying and distribution without permission of the copyright holder or payment to same. The United States copyright law states:

> *Notwithstanding the provisions of sections 106 and 106A (17 USC) the Fair Use of a copyrighted work, including such use by reproduction in copies or phonorecords or by any other means specified by that section, for purposes such as criticism, comment, news reporting, teaching (including multiple copies for classroom use), scholarship, or research, is not an infringement of copyright.*

As written, the language of this statute does not specifically define Fair Use, but it does provide an outline of non-exclusive factors to consider in determining Fair Use: how the work is used, how much of the work is used, and how does the use affect the value and potential sales of the original work. Those factors have been interpreted to include:

1. *The purpose and character of the use, including whether such use is of a commercial nature or is for nonprofit educational purposes;*

   Beyond the statutory categories such as scholarship, news etc., and perhaps of greater importance, is the use for commercial or non-commercial ends?

2. *The nature of the copyrighted work;*

   Is the material sought to be used as fiction or non-fiction? More protection is accorded works of fiction and imagination than works of non-fiction.

3. *The amount and substantiality of the portion used in relation to the copyrighted work as a whole;*

   Although some publishers or other owners fix a word limit, do not be misled into believing any use within that word limit is fair. Nor may you use the material on the cover of the work nor use the material in any way that gives it greater prominence than the rest of the work.

4. *The effect of the use upon the potential market for or value of the copyrighted work.*

The author or publisher who uses the material certainly would claim that its use enhances sales of the material because readers might be inclined to then purchase the work containing the copyrighted material that previously they perhaps would not have known about. The courts look to see if the copy is a substitute for the protected work, thereby depriving the owner of the protected work of some economic benefit. And this category relates to the previous one in that if you use the material in such a way as to give it more prominence, you may be depleting the value of the protected work.

An infringement suit with a somewhat unexpected outcome occurred when the rap group Two Live Crew deliberately copied part of the song "Pretty Woman," by Roy Orbison. The group had initially requested a license from Acuff-Rose, the music publisher, but the request was denied on the grounds that the new version demeaned the value of the copyright. The trial court ruled that the Two Live Crew version of the song was a parody, and as such, a use protected under the Fair Use doctrine. The case was appealed to the U.S. Supreme Court, which upheld the Fair Use, and claimed that the new version was a conscious transformation of the original, and fell within the protected category of a parody. This case also established that, under certain circumstances, even a commercial usage may fall within the protection of the Fair Use provisions.

Making one complete copy of a work—or using a portion of it for commercial purposes—is not considered Fair Use. The Digital Millennium Copyright Act prohibits the manufacture, importation, or distribution of devices whose intended use, or only significant commercial use, is to bypass a copy control mechanism put in place by a copyright owner. An appellate court has held that Fair Use is not a defense to engage in such distribution.

Fairness in Music Licensing Act

Notwithstanding the copyright provisions of section 106, the Fairness in Music Licensing Act (FMLA) of 1998 (17 U.S.C., Section 110), establishes guidelines for exemptions and limitations on certain performances and displays of copyrighted music. The following performances, under specific situations, may not be infringements of copyright:

1. performance or display of a work by instructors or pupils in the course of face-to-face teaching activities of an educational institution;
2. performance or transmission of a non-dramatic literary or musical work or display of a work of a religious nature, or display of a work, in the course of services at a place of worship or other religious assembly;
3. where the proceeds, after deducting the reasonable costs of producing the performance, are used exclusively for educational, religious, or charitable purposes and not for private financial gain;
4. performance of music in certain smaller bars and restaurants may be exempt from paying performance royalties.

The limitations of copyright protection which are established by the FMLA are technical provisions, and require the advice of an attorney before being exercised.

The First-Sale Doctrine

Copyright law does not restrict the owner of a copy from re-selling legitimately obtained copies of copyrighted works, provided that those copies were originally produced by or with the permission of the copyright holder. In the United States, this is known as the First-Sale Doctrine, and was established by the courts to clarify the legality of re-selling books in second-hand bookstores. In the 1976 Copyright Act, the doctrine was made to apply to any "owner" of a lawfully made copy or phonorecord. In situations where the copyright owner licenses someone to make a copy, that copy may lawfully be sold, lent, traded, or given away. Pursuant to the First-Sale Doctrine, therefore, it is legal to re-sell a copyrighted book or CD. It is important to note that the First-Sale Doctrine permits the transfer of the particular legitimate, original copy involved. It does not permit making or distributing additional copies of the original work.

Copyright infringement

MYTH-BUSTER: "Four bars are O.K. to use"

The notion has widely circulated among musicians that it is legal to copy "up to four bars" of music from someone else's work. There is nothing in the Copyright Act that allows this. Rumors that it is permissible to use so many notes or so many bars are simply not true. Rather than establishing any specific number of similar musical notes or bars, the courts have ruled that there are now two legal guidelines in determining whether one song infringes on an earlier copyrighted song: "substantial similarity" and "access." The word substantial should not be taken as a quantitative measure. A distinctive musical passage or lyric can consist of a small handful of notes that are recognizable. Ultimately, a judge, relying on expert opinions and solfeggists' (musicologists') analyses, makes a determination whether one song is "substantially similar" to another. The other aspect of an infringement suit, the issue of "access," requires that the person accused of the infringement, at some point in time, had access to the original song. This access may have been obtained through hearing a song on the radio, from owning a recording, or hearing a recording at a pitch session or other presentation. If the owner of a copyright can prove that a subsequent writer did, indeed, have an opportunity to hear the original piece of music, and that the subsequent work was "substantially similar" to the original work, a case can be made for copyright infringement.

There are a number of lawsuits that involve infringements that are especially well known. The late Beatle, George Harrison, was sued by the writers and publishers of a song called "He's So

Fine," which had been a hit during the 1950s for the Chiffons. Harrison's song, "My Sweet Lord," the plaintiffs showed, was virtually a note-for-note copy of "He's So Fine." Harrison lost the suit when it was proven that the song was played on the BBC when he was a teenager, and that he listened to the shows that had played it, establishing "access" to the original song.

Folksongs have historically been at the center of numerous infringement cases. Copyright controversies have erupted over the ownership rights to many iconic folksongs, including "500 Miles" and "Tom Dooley." The central question in these suits revolves around the creative contributions that the subsequent writers made to the historically traditional folksongs.

When a copyright suit is decided, penalties are harsher when it can be proven that the infringement of a copyrighted and registered work has been intentional. Such is the case when a subsequent writer contacts the original publisher, seeking permission to use or license the original work, but is denied the use of the song. In this regard, once the original publisher is aware of a potential derivative use, it becomes easier to establish that a derivative use was intentional. Even in those cases where intentional infringement is not established, the guilty party must credit the original writer and publisher on all future pressings of a record, and, of course, must also pay all received royalties for the use of the song back to the original owners.

Representatives: managers, lawyers

Mid-career, successful singer-songwriters generally are represented by a personal manager, a booking agent, a lawyer, and a business manager. All told, they may be commissioning nearly half of your gross income (the good news is that you have income!). Any other professionals that you need to utilize are generally paid on salaries. Some of the support crew might include a publicist, a road manager, any additional road crews (only if you become really successful) to help create your show, and so on. The artist's manager generally serves as the point person to help find all other career-support people through his network of personal contacts. As with any other successful business, as you grow, so do your expenses and costs of doing business.

Personal managers

The personal manager looks at an artist's long-term career goals, while a booking agent typically is focused on generating touring and performance dates. A competent personal manager will have numerous music industry contacts in the major music business cities, and will also help the artist to develop a broad career plan. Once an artist is signed to a record label deal, the manager's services include the following:

- liaison between the record company and the artist;
- deal maker and finder of new opportunities;
- promotional or marketing genius;
- central contact person who coordinates all artist activities;
- astute financial wizard who moves the artist into new creative endeavors;
- point person between the artist, the record producer, the record company, and booking agent.

The manager's role with the record label could be described as "working the record company." This means that the manager should be working hand-in-hand with the record company to develop and execute a promotional, marketing, and sales effort on behalf of the artist. With a constant eye on generating sales or downloads of an artist's recordings, a major objective for the manager becomes obtaining traditional radio airplay, as well as garnering advantageous Internet exposure. Records need to be promoted and available in stores when an artist is on tour. Window displays in record stores need to be similarly coordinated. The manager must coordinate and interface with each of the departments within the record company, constantly informing A&R people and marketing executives about the artist's achievements, great reviews, tour routings, successful appearances, and so on.

The manager should be developing the artist's career into new areas, including film and television placements, commercial and advertising opportunities, video game placements, and the emerging new media markets (website presence, digital download sales, ringtone and ringback opportunities, and fan-base connections). The manager should be seeking out meetings with television and filmmakers in Hollywood and New York, making directors and producers aware of the artist's ability to craft songs for films, television shows, and commercials. The financial piece of the puzzle involves expanding the artist's opportunities into such ancillary areas as merchandise, toys, endorsement deals for musical equipment, and even the world of fashion and life-style marketing. And in conjunction with the record label and the booking agent, the manager should assist in devising national and international promotional and touring campaigns that capitalize on the artist's talents. The personal manager is clearly a key person in the artist's career.

A manager's commission is entirely negotiable, and typically ranges from 10 to 20 percent of an artist's gross entertainment income. Although a manager's commission is usually applied against all of the standard "gross income" earnings of the artist (artist royalties, tour income, merchandise, and publishing), the "songwriter share" royalties are generally exempt from inclusion. The commission range will also vary based upon the profile and experience of the manager. The term of a management agreement usually consists of an initial contract period and one or more option periods. These periods may comprise either a number of years or "album cycles," if the artist is signed to a record deal. In rare circumstances, the term of a management agreement will be "at will" and each party will be entitled to terminate the agreement upon thirty days prior written notice. The initial contract period under a management agreement is generally for three to five years, or two album cycles. Option periods, which are exercisable in the manager's sole discretion, are usually for two years, or one to two additional album cycles.

Finding a manager or attorney

Unfortunately, merely identifying a talented manager or attorney to represent your act can be a hurdle in the development of your career. The top managers and attorneys can be as difficult to reach as major-label A&R execs, but the means of finding them is similar: research, references, and networking. Personal references are generally the best route to finding a good candidate. Ask other writers or performers you know for references for good managers and music attorneys. If you are friends with other artists in your hometown (especially those who are further along in their career than you are), start with them—they may be able to recommend attorneys they have already worked with and trust. Finding a manager is not an easy task, particularly if you live outside the music business mainstream. The magazine *The Music Connection* publishes a list of personal managers, and updates it on a quarterly basis. It is a great resource, but many of the managers listed are based in Los Angeles.

Once you've compiled a list of managers you'd like to approach for representation, send out presentation packages soliciting their representation. Have patience and stay with it. What you are looking for is a hard-working and trustworthy person who merits your confidence. The things you want to know from a prospective manager are:

- What other acts has she managed?
- What record deals has she made?
- What is the fee and expense structure?
- Is there an "out-clause," or performance standards that must be met by the manager?
- What are the specific tactics and strategies that the manager will employ to promote your career?

Keep in mind that just as with any other member of your team, there are tradeoffs between different levels of managers (and attorneys). For the most part, the really high-powered, well-known managers are not going to be able to devote the same kind of time and attention to developing artists that a lesser-known and younger manager will. If the manager has dealt with other acts, he should be able to provide you with references. If the manager has never shopped for a record deal before, what makes you think that he is capable of finding you one? Having said this, a young and hungry manager may well have the patience and stubbornness to pursue a record deal, and to find one, despite his lack of experience. Similarly, an experienced manager who is not hungry may not put forth much effort on your behalf. Many young artists make the mistake of choosing a "manager" who is simply a personal friend or a fan, rather than a professional. It is quite understandable that they would do so, because emerging artists usually lack significant contacts with anyone in the business. Artists should be particularly wary about confusing a personal friendship or relationship with a business deal. This is even more apt to be true if the artist lives in a city that is far removed from the music industry itself. The problem for the aspiring artist is that once you have signed a written contract, you have to live with it. This means that if you want to fire the manager at a later date as your career develops, you will have to reach a negotiated financial settlement with him. This may mean that you will be obligated to pay commissions to the fired manager, even though he is no longer working for you. And should your career continue to be successful, you will need to hire a new manager. Paying commissions to both an old and a new manager is a heavy burden to bear. A "sunset clause" in your management agreement addresses this problem (see below).

Managers as publishers

There are many instances where a manager will suggest that she and a songwriter or artist/writer should co-own a publishing company. If this occurs, be careful that the manager does not share in your publishing rights, and then, additionally take her commission from your songwriting income. This can be construed as double-dipping, and should be negotiated with caution.

Business managers

Successful singer-songwriters will also need to hire a business manager. Involved primarily with the financial, royalty, and tax aspects of an artist's career, business managers rarely become involved in the creative aspects. Business managers put an artist's financial affairs on a rational, professional course. This involves keeping tax records, paying taxes, making investments, and verifying royalty statements and distributions from record companies, publishing companies, and merchandising deals. As royalties and income increase, the use of a business manager becomes essential. In an effort to manage the long-term financial aspects of an artist's career, a business manager will often put the artist on a salary basis, and ensure that money is set aside for taxes and conservative investments which will secure her future. Once again, the more the artist knows and understands about these business decisions, the more likely the artist is to be protected against rash or foolish moves.

Entertainment attorneys

The simple rule of thumb about when a songwriter needs a music business attorney: the moment when a written agreement is offered. If you are inclined to sign a contract of any kind, you should have an attorney who understands the music business represent you and protect your interests. It is important that you find an experienced entertainment attorney, as opposed to a friend-of-the-family lawyer whose practice may consist of divorces or real estate law. The language of law (and especially entertainment law) is intricate, and you should never try to interpret it yourself. In other words, a careful study of music industry books may be sufficient to provide an overview and a basic understanding of the music business, but any binding, written agreement for services, songs, performances, payments, or income should always be reviewed by a music industry attorney.

A music attorney is a crucial member of any artist's team, and is also part of a larger entertainment industry network, consisting of relationships and contacts to record labels, booking agencies, management firms, and publishing companies. An entertainment attorney can play a significant role in advancing an artist's career, and, in this regard, the evaluation and selection of an attorney is just as important as evaluating a publisher, manager, or any other business partner. Ask what other clients the attorney represents, get references, and attempt to ascertain whether the attorney understands what you are trying to do with your overall career goals. The artist's attorney should not, in most cases, also be representing the artist's manager. The potential for a conflict of interest is very real, and barring unique situations, your attorney should be unrelated to your manager's business interests.

Compensation for an attorney's services can vary widely, as there are three basic fee structures that can be charged to developing artists: (1) a flat rate per contract; (2) an hourly fee; or (3) a percentage deal. The attorney will generally propose his preferred method of compensation, but the artist may be able to negotiate a favorable arrangement if there are lucrative third-party recording or publishing offers on the table. It is not unusual for an attorney to charge $300.00 per hour to negotiate and draft a recording Agreement, or, in the alternative, to take compensation in the form of 5 or 10 percent "of the deal." As the attorney fees can be significant in either case, it is important that the artist and attorney have a truthful and trusting relationship at the very outset of their association.

In looking for legal representation, another possible resource is the Volunteer Lawyers for the Arts (VLA). Based in New York, the VLA offers low-cost or free legal services throughout the United States, with fees based on the income of the client, rather than on set rates. The VLA offers a wide range of services including: consultations and referrals to other attorneys; a legal hotline; in-house appointments with VLA staff attorneys; and pro bono placements for low-income artists and nonprofit arts organizations (www.vlany.org; 212·319·ARTS).

If the singer-songwriter becomes successful, her earnings may now be commissioned as follows:

- manager: 20 percent
- business manager: 5 percent
- attorney: 5 percent.

Thirty percent is a significant portion of gross earnings.

Attorney and manager red flags

Since managers (and some attorneys) get a percentage of the deal that is structured, they may seek large advances for their clients, rather than escalating percentages of record royalties. The rationale for this is that if the artist gets a $100,000.00 advance, that means $20,000.00 for the manager's commission, and $5,000.00 for the attorney's fee, all paid up-front, out of the initial advance. A smaller advance with higher royalty percentages later will only generate significant royalties and fees if the artist sells a lot of CDs. If your business team is on your side, they should not be concerned with the short-term outlook and quick commissions, but they should be involved with representing your long-term interests.

Another red flag is that sometimes managers and lawyers have other artists under contract to the same record company, or artists that they are attempting to sign to that company. If you sense that your team isn't fighting hard enough for your crucial deal point, it may be that the attorney doesn't wish to antagonize the record company over your deal points, for fear of losing other deals for her other artists. Although these situations are rare, they do present potential conflicts of interest which can negatively impact an artist's career. It is therefore critical that the artist trusts his representatives, and understands the major aspects of the recording contract, such as royalty percentages and publishing rights, so that he is confident that he is being fairly and aggressively represented.

Another possible problem occurs when the manager is acting as the artist's record producer. In the case of Bruce Springsteen, his manager, Mike Appel, was also commissioning Bruce's record royalties. This meant that he may have been making more money from Bruce's records than Bruce was getting. Mike also was the publisher of Bruce's music. When Springsteen wanted to end his relationship with Appel, Columbia Records had to inform Bruce that they could not continue to make his records until the dispute was settled, for the simple reason that their contract was not with Bruce, but with Mike Appel. Unfortunately we are aware of other stories of a similar nature. Although the vast majority of representatives are honest, ethical, and have their artist's best interests in mind, it is wise to be alert to any sort of double dipping that your manager or music business attorney may be engaged in.

Contract clauses

"Power of Attorney" clause

A "Power of Attorney" (PoA) is a document or clause that establishes a relationship between a writer and a publisher, wherein the writer "designates, empowers, and appoints the publisher" to represent the writer in specific contract, copyright, and licensing situations. The publisher is, therefore, authorized to act on the writer's behalf to conduct those acts which are necessary and appropriate to protect or enhance the writer's (and publisher's) interests. The PoA is an acceptable clause in a publishing agreement—when limited to copyright and licensing issues involving the writer's works—and serves to greatly facilitate procedural licensing, placement, and royalty collection issues. Although this clause allows the publisher considerable latitude to file registrations and enter into song licenses, a writer typically reserves the right to personally approve sensitive or political uses of the songs.

Key Man clause

Another protection in a publishing or recording agreement that the writer-artist can seek is known as a "Key Man" clause. This clause states that if the primary creative person (Key Man) who brought the writer into the company should leave the company for any reason, then the artist can choose to terminate the commitment to the company, without penalty. Many times, a writer or artist will accept a long-term contract with a company based on the personal relationship that is developed with one key executive. Although it is not uncommon for executives and staff to leave one job for another, the personal relationship and artistic vision that is shared between a writer and a "champion at the company" can be a great inducement for an artist to sign a deal with one company over another. The Key Man clause, although very difficult to obtain, would allow a writer to end a contractual relationship if certain key figures no longer worked at the company.

Right of Publicity

The Right of Publicity is most commonly defined as the right of every individual to control the commercial use of his or her name, image, likeness, or some other identifying aspect of his or her identity. The Right of Publicity can be referred to as "publicity rights" or even "personality rights." Protecting the individual from the loss of commercial value resulting from the unauthorized appropriation of an individual's identity for commercial purposes is the principle purpose of these laws.

Until relatively recently, the Right of Publicity only applied to deceased people. It also used to be quite common for people who sang on commercials to imitate both existing styles and existing stylists. Both Tom Waits and Bette Midler have won landmark law suits over the use of their vocal styles in commercials. In Midler's case, the advertising agency had tried unsuccessfully to hire her to do a commercial. When she refused, the agency hired a vocalist who had been a back-up singer in Midler's shows. Waits, on the other hand, has a rather unusual vocal style, and has long been known as being opposed to the notion of appearing in or performing for commercials. He sued when an agency hired someone to imitate his vocal sound in a commercial. Both of these cases were won by the artists, on grounds that their personal Right of Publicity was violated, and since that time agencies have become more careful about literally imitating other people's sounds.

Most Favored Nations clause

In entertainment agreements, a Most Favored Nations (MFN) clause provides that a license fee, a royalty rate, or another aspect of a contractual relationship will be computed in "as favorable a manner" as the fees given to one or more third parties involved in the same project. The MFN clause streamlines the negotiation process, and assures all participants that they are on equal footing with all other third parties. If you are a music publisher and have a song in a movie or television production, it is logical to have concerns that your particular song is not being compensated as well as another publisher's songs. This concern is resolved by a MFN clause. This clause states that no other song in the film or project can receive more money than your song is getting. It takes care of the situation very neatly, and is often demanded by music publishers.

There are several reasons why one or both parties would wish to have an MFN clause. The clause can eliminate significant transaction and negotiation costs in both time and money by establishing a clearly defined level of compensation for all contributors. By standing firm on the MFN terms, however, the production company must be willing to lose content or services from third parties who may refuse to accept that level of compensation. MFN clauses also provide licensors and other royalty recipients the comfort of knowing that no one else will be treated in a more favorable manner with respect to a particular term. This assurance is a security blanket for publishers who can assure their writers that a particular license fee is the best available for the project in question.

MFN clauses can be particularly helpful to parties with small bargaining leverage confronted by lengthy standard terms. In the case of deal terms covering license fees for song placements in a motion picture, studio boilerplate language is often extremely long, and if every clause were negotiated, transaction costs would be extremely high for both parties. MFN clauses are also used when a compilation CD is assembled in which rights are sought from various record companies. The company assembling the compilation record may reduce the time and trouble of negotiation by assuring all licensors that they will receive the same license fee, or royalty rate. Both the licensor and the licensee stand to benefit from the appropriate use of MFN treatment.

Sunset clause

A "sunset clause" is the contract tool used to determine how much compensation is owed to a manager (or attorney), should the parties agree to stop working together following a long association. Whatever the reason for a split between a music manager and an artist, both parties should protect themselves from unfair exploitation by adopting a sunset clause in their music management contract. A sunset clause recognizes the contribution that a manager has made to an artist's career, while establishing a "post-employment" commission structure that leaves the door open for the artist to be able to afford to hire different managers or professionals at a later stage in her career. In most cases, the "sunset" refers to the amount of commissions that will be paid to a former manager over the years following a split. A sunset clause typically grants the former manager full commission for six months following the split, reduced by a third every six months, until the former manager can no longer claim a commission. The income distributed to the manager generally derives from: (1) the deals signed by the artist prior to the termination; and (2) the deals which were substantially negotiated by the manager prior to the termination, and which resulted in a completed contract after the termination.

Without a sunset clause, an artist could split with her manager, but still be liable for paying commissions as long as they were being generated. The sunset clause forces both parties to take their relationship seriously, while allowing for the possibility that an artist and her manager might grow apart before the end of their agreed-upon contract term. For further details, consult co-author Dick Weissman's best-selling book, *The Music Business: Career Opportunities & Self Defense*, third revised edition.

13 Music organizations and resources

Making use of songwriter organizations

Most cities in the United States now have a local or regional songwriter organization. These groups generally sponsor monthly meetings where various writers present their songs, which are critiqued by other songwriters. Such organizations are great places to meet other songwriters and potential collaborators. Many of these groups also bring in well-known writers or music publishers to conduct seminars on various songwriting subjects, or to critique songs. This provides the members with an opportunity to get professional feedback without having to visit the major music cities. If one of these visiting professionals takes an interest in your material, they may be able to provide you with invaluable contacts in the music publishing and recording industry. Listening to the work of other songwriters and sharing mutual interests, concerns, successes, and failures can be a great learning experience for a songwriter. As many songwriters work alone, these meetings provide an opportunity to share your work, and to interact with a supportive community.

Organizations that cover specific genres of music

There are national music organizations that cover virtually every style of music, and in many instances there are local or state-wide organizations that also focus on various genres. These groups are of particular importance if you are writing in a specialized field of music, such as bluegrass, country, or jazz. Membership in a genre-based organization can provide enormous benefits, tools, and contacts for an emerging artist's career. A web search will lead you to music organizations in virtually every genre of music, including polka music, or Native American music and their annual Nammy Awards ceremony. If you are writing songs in a particular genre, it is essential that you become aware of opportunities in that specific field of music.

National Association of Music Merchandisers (NAMM)

The National Association of Music Merchandisers (NAMM) includes manufacturers and wholesalers of musical instruments, and the owners of retail music stores. NAMM produces a large winter trade show in January, in Anaheim, California, and a summer show, in July, which has moved from Nashville to Indianapolis to Austin. All of the major music print publishers have large exhibits at NAMM, and they write a substantial percentage of their annual business at the winter show. To promote their products, the merchandisers offer special discounts and a wide range of promotional items, and the major print publishers, including Mel Bay, Music Sales, and Hal Leonard exhibit their song catalogue and folios through print and on line offerings.

If you are interested in writing about the music business, or have any ideas for writing articles for the print and book publishers, NAMM provides an opportunity to meet the people who work at these companies. It is often better to initiate contacts at NAMM rather than to try to pitch them on your ideas, because the primary reason for the music merchants to attend the show is to sell products to music stores. The summer show has less traffic, and is probably a better place to make contacts. The NAMM trade show is a great place to learn about the academic, retail, and instrument part of the music business. Although NAMM is not open to the public, you can get a visitor's badge through one of your local music stores, many of which attend the show. Tickets may also be available through the National Academy of Recording Arts and Sciences (NARAS), or through the music industry programs at various colleges throughout the country that teach music merchandising courses (see www.namm.org).

National Academy of Recording Arts and Sciences (NARAS)

Although NARAS is best known for producing the annual Grammy Awards television show, this organization can be very useful for artists or songwriters intent on making professional contacts on a local or regional level. Over the last ten years, NARAS has developed a strong regional presence, with chapters having been created in Austin, Philadelphia, Seattle, and Washington D.C., as well as its long-standing chapters in Atlanta, Chicago, Los Angeles, Memphis, Minneapolis, Nashville, and New York.

As is the case with local songwriting organizations, NARAS provides an opportunity to meet other songwriters, as well as musicians, recording engineers, and record producers. There are chapter meetings and various educational programs as well. In order to become a voting member of NARAS, the applicant has to have six credits on recordings in national release. These are all credits in the creative aspects of recording, including liner notes, performing as an artist, back-up singer, or musician, writing songs, or creating album covers. For those who don't meet these criteria, associate memberships are available. Each local chapter of the organization has an Executive Director, and you are encouraged to check out the chapter's activities to determine whether membership will be worthwhile for you (see www. grammy.com).

Nashville Songwriters Association International (NSAI)

The Nashville Songwriters Association International (NSAI) is the only national songwriters' organization active today. The organization includes songwriters from all genres of music, professional and amateur, and (1) operates as a legislative advocacy group on behalf of songwriters, (2) teaches writers about the "craft" of writing, and (3) produces instructional seminars about the music industry, how it works, and how a songwriter or artist can position himself and his songs for success within the industry. NSAI has two levels of activity. For the Nashville-area songwriter, the organization provides professional industry contacts, writing rooms, intensive educational seminars and presentations, and is a tremendous resource for the songwriting community. NSAI's expanded online services provide virtual accessibility to members living outside of Nashville, where writer members can access the NSAI song evaluation service, live chats with pro writers, instructional forums, live and archived workshops/ classes, and more than one hundred regional workshops. If you are writing in the country genre, membership of NSAI is highly recommended (see www.nashvillesongwriters.com).

Country Music Association (CMA)

The CMA was founded in 1959, and is a powerful trade organization with over 5,500 members. There are more than twenty categories of membership ranging from artists, to songwriters, to recording engineers. In addition to their prestigious annual CMA awards program, the organization sponsors a huge event called Fan Fair, where fans can meet and interact on a one-to-one basis with their favorite artists. Various publications, including a guide to country music radio stations, and a scholarly quarterly magazine that discusses everything from the history of the genre to current controversies in country music, are part of the organization's work. The CMA also produces re-issue recordings of historical importance, and maintains a museum that is part tourist attraction and part scholarly home to out-of-print recordings, posters of old concerts, and various country music memorabilia. The CMA can be a valuable networking resource for songwriters, especially those who live in the Nashville area (see www.cmaworld.com).

Academy of Country Music (ACM)

This is a somewhat smaller organization than the CMA, and was founded in Los Angeles in 1964. It focuses on an annual awards ceremony, and is more oriented towards contemporary country music than CMA's combined historical and contemporary approach (see www.acmcountry.com).

International Bluegrass Music Association (IBMA)

Bluegrass musicians gather for the annual IBMA meeting in Nashville each September. Since many bluegrass musicians do not write songs, or write only occasionally, the annual meeting is an excellent opportunity to find artists in the genre who are seeking new songs. The meeting is also kind of a miniature NAMM trade show, where musical instrument manufacturers and boutique luthiers showcase their instruments and products, along with record companies, disc jockeys, and print publishers that specialize in bluegrass music. IBMA also has a Bluegrass Awards show as part of the annual conference. Many states have bluegrass associations which publish newsletters and enable writers to meet local performing artists who may be a target market for new songs (see www.ibma.org).

North American Folk Music and Dance Alliance

The Folk Alliance is a loose confederation of folk music and dance presenters, musicians, songwriters, performers, agents, managers, disc jockeys, folk dance enthusiasts, and record companies who conduct business in North America. Formed in 1989, and including more than 2,400 members, the Folk Alliance goals are aimed at increasing access to needed resources for the membership, and to expand the breadth of the folk music and dance experience for the general public.

There is an annual meeting held in February in Memphis four out of five years. The fifth year the meeting is held in Canada, because the membership includes many Canadians. The February meeting has become the "town hall" of the folk community, where nearly 2,000 members attend each year to conduct business and connect with their peers. The annual meeting is, in effect, the world's largest acoustic jam session. There are official and guerrilla showcases where artists can perform and showcase their work. For a songwriter, there is exposure to peers and professionals coming from across North America. There are also panels on the folk music business, promotion, marketing, and the history of folk music in North America. In addition to the national meeting, the organization also has regional sub-chapters in the Northeast, and the West Coast. Both the national and regional meetings present awards for people associated with folk music as performers or promoters of the music. These are lifetime achievement awards, and are not based on accomplishments occurring during the prior year (see www.folkalliance.org).

Gospel Music Association (GMA)

This organization has been in existence since 1964. Members include artists, record executives, radio stations, concert promoters, and churches. The purpose of the organization is to promote the Christian music industry, which unlike most of the music industry continues to enjoy steady growth. In April of each year, the GMA holds a week of seminars and concerts, and presents their annual Dove Awards, honoring the outstanding Christian artists, songs, and records of the previous year. During the summer of each year, the GMA presents a "Music in the Rockies" showcase event for songwriters and artists in the Christian music industry. The event takes place at the YMCA Camp in Estes Park, Colorado. The GMA has also created a Hall of Fame, which recognizes major artists ranging from Mahalia Jackson to Elvis Presley and the Blackwood Brothers (see www.gospelmusic.org).

California Copyright Conference (CCC)

The California Copyright Conference was established in Los Angeles, in 1953, to promote and encourage the discussion of copyright-related areas pertaining to music and entertainment. Today, the scope of the CCC has expanded to cover all matters pertaining to music industry issues. The CCC presents monthly meetings, open to the public, on selected Tuesdays, featuring prominent guest speakers or an industry panel discussion. The meetings cover a broad range of subjects of interest to the music industry, as well as regular "legal updates" on current litigation and legislation that affects the industry. Recent topics have included Fair Use and parody, film and television music, soundtrack albums, independent record labels, getting songs on the radio, music agents, publishers and labels, interactive technology, and the challenges of the Internet (see www.theccc.org).

Association of Independent Music Publishers (AIMP)

The Association of Independent Music Publishers (AIMP) was formed in 1977 by a group of Los Angeles music publishers, and now operates chapters in both Los Angeles and New York. The organization's primary focus is to educate and inform local music publishers about current industry trends and practices by providing a forum for the discussion of the issues confronting the music publishing industry.

The AIMP provides a unique medium for those in the music industry to discuss various points of view from the cutting edge of the ever-changing music business. The opportunity to exchange ideas and opinions with others on issues of mutual concern is fostered by the informal atmosphere of the AIMP's monthly meetings, forums, and workshops, all of which are open to the public.

The AIMP includes in its membership independent music publishers, as well as major music publishers that are affiliated with record labels or motion picture and television production companies. In addition, individuals from other areas of the entertainment community, including multimedia and home video producers, the record industry, music licensing and supervision, songwriters, artist managers, and members of the legal and accounting professions, are active in the AIMP (see www.aimp. org).

South by Southwest Music Conference (SXSW)

The first South by Southwest Music Conference and Festival (SXSW) was held in 1987 in Austin, Texas. Since 1987, SXSW has produced the internationally recognized Music and Media Conference and Festival each year, in March. In 1994, SXSW added conferences and festivals for the film industry, SXSW Film, as well as for the emerging interactive media market, SXSW Interactive Festival. All three festivals take place in one week in March, in Austin. In addition to the SXSWeek events in Austin, SXSW is also involved in producing North by Northeast (NXNE), held in Toronto, Canada in late spring.

Attracting more than 7,000 annual attendees, the SXSW Music and Media Conference showcases hundreds of musical acts from around the globe on over fifty stages in downtown Austin. By day, conference registrants do business in the SXSW trade show in the Austin Convention Center, and can attend of a full agenda of panel discussions featuring hundreds of speakers of international stature. The SXSW Interactive Festival showcases the creativity behind the newest new media technologies. In addition to panel sessions that cover everything from web design to bootstrapping to social networks, attendees make new business connections at the three-day trade show and Exhibition. And the SXSW Film Conference and Festival emphasizes all aspects of the art and business of independent filmmaking. The Festival has gained international acclaim for the quality of its programming, with a special focus on emerging talents (see www.sxsw.com).

Music and Entertainment Industry Educators Association (MEIEA)

The Music and Entertainment Industry Educators Association is an international organization, formed in 1979, to bring together educators with leaders of the music and entertainment industries. The primary goal of MEIEA is to facilitate an exchange of information between educators and practitioners in order to prepare students for careers in the music and entertainment industries.

MEIEA endeavors to: (1) provide resources for the exchange of information and knowledge about all aspects of the music and entertainment industries; (2) foster scholarly research on the music and entertainment industries as well as on music and entertainment industries education; (3) assist institutions with the development of music and entertainment industries programs and curricula; (4) facilitate interaction between the music and entertainment industries and music and entertainment industries' educators and affiliated educational institutions; and (5) promote student interests in the music and entertainment industries through guidance and support of the Music and Entertainment Industry Student Association (MEISA) (see www.meiea.org).

American Music Center (AMC)

If you write music that falls into the genre of classical music, the American Music Center is a tremendous resource. The AMC was founded in 1939 by six contemporary classical music composers, including Aaron Copland. The Center sponsors a web magazine, a twenty-four-hour online radio station, and administers $1.5 million in grants to individuals and organizations involved in the composition, recording, and distribution of contemporary classical music. Among the Center's many resources is the New Music Jukebox, which is an online data base of over 40,000 works by American composers. Some of the other AMC publications, available by subscription, include online directories of ensembles and compositional opportunities in new music (see www.amc.net).

Taxi

Taxi is an independent music services company that performs song pitching and A&R functions. It was founded in 1992, and it operates like a record company in the sense that it screens and critiques the work of songwriters and prospective recording artists. For an annual fee, currently $300.00, with renewals priced at $200.00, a songwriter or artist can have her song critiqued by one of a panel of over 2,100 experts. Many of these people are former record or publishing company executives, and because the group is so large, virtually every imaginable musical genre is represented. Taxi promises to send each member listings of film music supervisors, TV producers, record company personnel, and other people who are working on specific projects and looking for material or for artists. The company brochure promises to send each member 1,200 of these opportunities each year. To have a song critiqued, a member pays an additional fee of $5.00 per song. The critiques are written, and cover very specific questions, with each expert working from an outline to ensure that the writer is given a thorough response to her song. If the panelist is enthusiastic about the song, he may pass it on to one of his contacts in the industry

Taxi also produces an annual Road Rally, a three-day convention that features many music industry panels, and also offers members a chance to perform live before an audience of 2,000 Taxi members. A monthly newsletter, available only to members, contains interviews with articles about people working in the business. If you live outside of the music business centers, Taxi is a good means of obtaining professional song critiques, and of getting your songs in the hands of music supervisors (see www. taxi.com).

Songwriting contests

There are numerous songwriting contests throughout the United States and many foreign countries. Some are local, some are regional, and some are international. The larger contests generally have three things in common: there is an entry fee, there are prizes awarded to the winner, and there are lots of submissions. These prizes range from monetary awards, to recording time at a major studio, to the award of musical instruments or recording gear, and even a record deal of some kind. Most of the contests will tell you that the quality of the demos is a secondary matter, that the qualified judges are capable of hearing a great song whether it is over- or under-produced. We take these claims with a grain of salt. If you are planning to enter a contest, make sure that the vocal is recorded cleanly and audibly, and that the singer delivers a great performance. For the typical songwriting contest, it isn't necessary to produce a master-quality recording, but a decent recording of a great song will surely help your chances to win.

Regional songwriting contests often feature the finalists in live appearances at music festivals, like the Kerrville Music Festival in Texas, or the Rocky Mountain Festival in Lyons, Colorado. From a songwriter's point of view, these "live performance contests" present a difficult dilemma: you may be a superior songwriter, but not an accomplished performer. Although your song may be the strongest, your chances of winning the "writing" contest may be greatly diminished in the live setting.

Songpluggers

If you are a songwriter who doesn't have a publisher, you may want to consider hiring an independent songplugger, or song-pitcher. A songplugger takes an unpublished song and attempts to get it recorded, or placed in a film or television production through his network of personal contacts. In return for these services, the songwriter either pays a flat fee or a percentage of what the song earns. If the song is extremely successful, the songplugger may also ask for part ownership of the copyright.

Basically, the services of these promoters are quite similar to what a professional manager does at a music publishing company. Instead of working for a company, the songplugger is essentially your employee. The effectiveness of this promotional avenue depends upon the skills, contacts, and enthusiasm of the person plugging the song. In the same way that you would seek references when hiring an attorney or a manager, it is advisable to check on the songplugger's track record with other songwriters, or by asking direct questions to the prospective plugger. If you are a member of one of the songwriter organizations, or one of the PROs, you should ask your contacts there what they know about the prospective plugger.

Negotiating a commission structure for a songplugger is not unlike any other fixed fee vs. percentage arrangement. The advantage of paying a flat fee is that you know exactly what it will cost you for these services. On the other hand, if you give up a percentage, it is impossible to predict what this is going to cost you in the long run.

Unions

The two unions that govern musical performers are the American Federation of Musicians (AFM) and the American Federation of Television and Radio Artists (AFTRA). The Screen Actors Guild (SAG) is a sister union of AFTRA, but is confined to the medium of film.

If you are a performing artist and sign a major label recording deal, your contract will compel you to join one of the two talent unions. They in turn will set minimum payments for recording sessions, and for other professional situations. Many of these minimums are quite high, and musicians who utilize them receive various bonuses based upon the gross revenues of an individual film, in the case of film recording, or the sales of all recordings, in the case of recording contracts. Similar rules apply to commercials that run for more than thirteen weeks.

American Federation Of Musicians (AFM)

If you are a touring or recording musician who expects to pursue a career on a long-term basis, there are many compelling reasons to join the AFM. If a club owner or venue operator fails to pay you for a performance, the union's "guaranteed contract clause" will pay you the union minimum wage, and then the union will take the club owner to court, at its expense. If the union recovers the entire sum of your wages (if you were contracted for over the minimum price scale) the union will pay you the remainder of the money when it recovers it in the court proceeding. There is also an 800 phone number which is answered on a twenty-four-hour basis, offering immediate assistance to all members. Other union programs offer pension contributions and musical instrument insurance. The union also can be a source of work, depending upon the particular union local involved (there are about 250 of them in the United States and Canada). In some cities, the union has an efficient full-time staff that is quite cooperative. In other cities, there may be one part-time official, who has another full-time job. Over the years, the AFM has become more oriented towards a regional service, and less towards a local one. The AFM also sets wage scales for recording albums, commercials, or for movie scores.

On the other hand, if you see performing as a very small sideline in a local market, the cost of union membership may exceed the value of getting a union card. To join, you need to pay an initiation fee, which ranges from a pittance to well over a hundred dollars in the larger locals, plus annual dues, which are priced similarly. There are also work dues, usually 2 to 3 percent of the union minimum wages, which apply against all performance income. If you are working regularly, union membership is cost effective, but if you do a gig a month or less, the price may exceed the value.

American Federation of Television and Radio Artists (AFTRA)

AFTRA operates on a regional basis, with offices in major cities. The initiation fees and dues are higher than they are for the AFM, but benefits are also more generous. If you earned $10,000.00 during four consecutive quarters of the year, you are eligible for individual health benefits. The AFTRA pay scales are higher than AFM scales, and the money paid for residuals can be substantial. The scales for commercials are based on the time buy, whether the commercial is local, regional, or national, and whether it is broadcast in prime time. Many AFTRA members are also involved in film, and they must join SAG. There is a discount for dual membership, but the fees are still rather high. If you become involved in singing back-up on major label records, or singing on commercials, joining AFTRA is certainly worthwhile. In many of the smaller local markets, commercials and voiceover work is done non-union, so that union membership may not be beneficial for you.

Arts organizations

Regional arts organizations are also places where singer-songwriters can showcase. The emphasis here is on local presenters, often connected with Arts Councils. These regional groups also publish directories of performers, and have workshops on various aspects of performing. If you are on their email list, from time to time they will send out emergency calls for performers when someone has canceled a performance at the last minute.

Grants, Arts Councils and teaching opportunities

Every state in the United States and every province in Canada has an Arts Council that provides grants to arts organizations and artists. Many of the states sponsor "Residencies" in their local schools, where a songwriter (or artist) is commissioned to teach classes about their particular specialty. Dick Weissman has conducted Residencies in Colorado and Oregon, and received a long-term grant to teach songwriting to teenagers in a lockup facility that served as a court-sponsored alternative to prison.

In order to obtain a grant, applicants generally have to fill out a form, describing the artistic endeavor or education that can be provided, and how the classes may benefit the local artists in that state. Grants are usually reviewed by authorities in the field, who may have specific questions about the qualifications of the applicant. The grants are then usually assigned numerical scores, based upon such criteria as serving disadvantaged urban or rural populations, seniors, residents of a halfway house, or projects aimed towards minority groups. Some grants involve travel, and may require the applicant to remain in a town for days, weeks, or even months, depending on the nature of the grant. If the applicant has received a grant that involves the teaching of songwriting, there may also be obligations to perform the songs written during the Residency. Additional information and publications about grants and Arts Councils can be found at the Foundation Center. There are also many family foundations throughout North America, which offer financial support for a number of different artistic or educational endeavors. Teaching songwriting is a unique endeavor, where writers may very well find that the process of analyzing and explaining the structure and content of songs to others will actually stimulate their own writing.

Special material

There are numerous ways of finding outlets for your songwriting abilities. Churches may be interested in commissioning a new folk mass or other music. If you are a regular churchgoer, check with your minister. Don't overlook other denominations. You can access them through friends who attend other churches. Cities sometimes commission songs that are intended to draw attention to themselves as attractive tourist destinations. This may occur when the city is celebrating an anniversary of its founding, or simply because the local chamber of commerce wants to attract attention to the town. Sometimes cities hold contests to determine the best song, and the winner gets a cash prize, and the song gets performed on several public occasions. If the song catches on, this may become a regular event.

Co-author Dick Weissman wrote a series of songs for towns in Colorado that were serviced by a particular bank. In one case, the bank was doing quite well and was celebrating the opening of a new branch. The town, however, was rather depressed, with boarded up store windows and out-migration exceeding people moving in. The bank sponsored a public performance of the song, and gave away a recording of the song at the opening. The bank liked the song so well that they commissioned two other versions of it for other towns in Colorado where they had branch banks. Because they didn't want to pay the same fee, Dick ended up using the same tune with different lyrics for the other two banks. One of the banks then commissioned a choral arrangement of the song that was performed by a community choral group.

Books

There are many useful books available that detail the craft of songwriting. They can be quite useful as a source of inspiration. They tend to fall into several categories:

- books that offer details about how songs are constructed;
- books that are intended to teach the reader how to write hit songs;
- books that are essentially autobiographical works by song-writers;
- books that focus on the creative aspects of songwriting;
- books that focus on the business aspects of songwriting;
- collections of interviews with well-known songwriters.

Each of these books may have their uses, depending upon the extent of your current knowledge base. Song construction texts may offer tips about rhyme schemes, or how melodies are constructed and chords are utilized. The books that promise to help you write hit songs are probably the least useful, because the writing process continually evolves, and these books tend to be focused on past songs rather than current hits. Autobiographical works may offer inspiration, but what works for one writer may not be that useful for another one. The books that offer tips on creativity can be useful because they offer approaches used by different writers, and tips on what to do when inspiration seems to fail you. Since this happens to everyone sooner or later, it is a dilemma you will ultimately have to face. The business aspects of songwriting, like most of this book, focus on copyrighting, publishing, and royalties. Certainly a songwriter needs to be informed about these matters. The value of the interview collections depends upon the skills of the interviewer in convincing the songwriter to divulge some of her personal secrets of the trade. The books that are of most practical use are written by authors who have an almost encyclopedic knowledge of the songs written by the writers interviewed. This tends to take the conversations out of the superficial aspects of the craft. Under those circumstances, the writers share an in-depth analysis of their writing techniques, goals, successes and frustrations.

Periodicals and reference materials

In addition to the many newsletters published by local songwriting groups, there are two magazines that regularly provide songwriters with relevant articles about contemporary songwriting and music publishing: *American Songwriter* and *Performing Songwriter*. The latter magazine is aimed specifically at singer-songwriters rather than pure songwriters. Both magazines offer articles on music publishers, the state of the industry, and songcraft.

The last word

By the time this book is in the reader's hand, mechanical royalty payments will have increased to the new 2008 rate, generating additional income to songwriters and music publishers. Singer-songwriters will certainly benefit from the ever-increasing number of live music venues. The Internet and digital tools will increasingly allow rural artists to sell their music to foreign countries. Many writers will sign with smaller independent labels, release and distribute recordings on their own, or even develop an ownership role in their own record company. A growing number of writer-artists, typified by Ani DiFranco (Righteous Babe Records) and Conor Oberst (Bright Eyes), either operate their own labels, or create unique licensing and distribution partnerships for domestic and foreign sales of their music.

The market for music has become increasingly a world market, rather than one that is centered in the United States, and anchored to major label releases, and major market airplay. And it is unclear if the major record companies will ever recover their income and singular dominance in the entertainment industry. The business of music publishing, however, constitutes one of the bright spots in the industry. Notwithstanding the obvious challenges that illegal file sharing and piracy pose to music publishers and songwriters, the growing use of songs and instrumental music in television, commercials, film, and numerous emerging digital and ancillary markets has created expanding revenue streams for music publishers and songwriters.

Despite the threats and challenges, technological advances and new media opportunities have ushered in entirely new income streams for creators. It is clear that the cell phone and the computer will become major sources for the distribution of music. Apple's iPhone is just one of several emerging devices which incorporate cell phone functionality with enormous digital music and storage capabilities. The expanding royalty scenario for copyright owners bodes well for the long-range viability of composers and publishers.

In this book we have explored the origins and evolution of the modern world of music publishing. It is our hope that the book has been enjoyable and easy to read. If you are a young songwriter or singer-songwriter, many decisions await you in terms of figuring out the best way to take your music into a marketplace that will enable you to lead a creatively fulfilling and rewarding career. We wish you the best of success. The Bibliography has numerous resources—books and websites that are designed for those who want further information about the contemporary world of music publishing. You can reach the authors through this book's publisher, or go to their websites. The website for Ron Sobel's company, *North Star Media*, is www.northstarmedia. com, and you can find Dick Weissman on the Net at www. dickweissman.com.

Bibliography

Books

Note: There are countless books available on the subject of songwriting. Since this is primarily a book that concerns music publishing, we have not listed these works.

Adams, Ramsey, Avid Hantlik and David Weiss. *Music Supervision: The Complete Guide to Selecting Movies, TV, Game and New Media.* New York: Schirmer Trade Books, 2005.

Beall, Eric. *Making Music Make Money: An Insider's Guide to Becoming Your Own Music Publisher.* Boston, MA: Berklee Press, 2004.

Brabec, Jeff and Todd Brabec. *Music, Money and Success: The Insider's Guide to Making Money in the Music Industry.* New York: Schirmer Trade Books, 2006 (revised about every two years).

Braheny, John. *The Craft and Business of Songwriting.* 3rd ed. Cincinnati: Writer's Digest, 2006.

Demers, Joanna. *Steal his Music; How Intellectual Property Law Affects Musical Creativity.* Athens, GA: University of Georgia Press, 2006.

Frith, Simon and Lee Marshall, eds. *Music and Copyright.* 2nd ed. New York: Routledge, 2007.

Gordon, Steve. *The Future of the Business: How to Succeed with the New Digital Technologies.* San Francisco: Back Bay Books, 2005.

Jay, Richard. *How to Get Your Music in Film and TV.* New York: Schirmer Trade Books, 2005.

Kusek, Dave and Gerd Leonhard. *The Future of Music: Manifesto for the Digital Music Revolution.* Boston: Berklee Music Press, 2005.

Lessig, Lawrence. *Free Culture: The Nature and Future of Creativity.* New York: Penguin Books, 2004.

May, Tom and Dick Weissman. *Promoting Your Music: The Lovin' of the Game.* New York: Routledge, 2007.

Moser, David J. *Music Copyright for the New Millennium.* Vallejo, CA: Pro Music Press, 2002.

Poe, Randy. *The New Songwriter's Guide to Music Publishing.* 3rd ed. Cincinnati: Writer's Digest Books, 2005.

Sanjek, Russell. *American Popular Music and Its Business; The First Four Hundred Years. Volume 1, The Beginning to 1790.* New York: Oxford University Press, 1988.

——*American Popular Music and Its Business: The First Four Hundred Years. Volume II, From 1790–1909.* New York: Oxford University Press, 1988.

Sanjek, Russell and David Sanjek. *American Popular Music Business in the 20th Century.* New York: Oxford University Press, 1991.

Songwriter's Market. Cincinnati: Writer's Digest, 1979– (published annually).

Weissman, Dick. *Songwriting: The Words, The Music and the Money.* Milwaukee: Hal Leonard, 2001.

——*The Music Business: Career Opportunities & Self Defense.* 3rd ed. New York: Three Rivers Press, 2003.

Whitsett, Tim. *Music Publishing: The Road to Music Business Success.* 5th ed. Vallejo, CA: Mix Books, 2005.

Wixen, Randall D. *The Plain and Simple Guide to Music Publishing.* Milwaukee: Hal Leonard, 2005.

Magazines

American Songwriter (www.americansongwriter.com)
Billboard (www.billboard.com)
Performing Songwriter (www.performingsongwriter.com)
The Music Connection (www.musicconnection.com)

Websites

AFM (American Federation of Musicians) www.afm.org
ASCAP (American Society of Composers, Authors, and Publishers) www.ascap.com
BMI (Broadcast Music Incorporated) www.bmi.com
SESAC (Society of European Stage Authors and Composers) www.sesac.com

Index

CPSIA information can be obtained at www.ICGtesting.com
Printed in the USA
BVOW08s1035220813

329228BV00008B/220/P